Clue of Ball Lightning puzzles

TORCHIGIN V. and TORCHIGIN A.

ISBN: 1511889438
ISBN-13: 9781511889438

CONTENTS

Introduction 5

What is Ball Lightning? 10

Laws of optics for explanation of the paradoxes 13

The answers to the riddles 17

    Overcoming Gravity 17

    Uniform horizontal movement 21

    Explanation bouncing 21

    Bypassing obstacles 22

    Why directions of the wind and a motion of the ball lightning can be
different 23

    Why ball lightning seems cold 25

    Explanation of circles inside perimeter 26

    Explanation of the ball lightning motion in a room near a floor rather than
near ceiling 27

    Explanation how the ball lightning finds out splits, holes, and chimneys to
penetrate through them 28

    Explanation of penetration in rooms through small splits and holes 29

    How the ball lightning enters the room through the window panes 34

    Behavior of the ball lightning near metal objects 45

    Why the ball lightning whistles and causes radio interference 48

    Why the ball lightning of large diameter takes the form of a flying saucer .. 49

        Why ball lightnings may have different colors 50

    The disappearance of ball lightning 50

    How the ball lightning is catching up a flying aircraft 51

Conclusion 61

References 62

Introduction

Mysterious natural phenomenon in the form of Ball Lightning (BL) is observed and studied by scientists for centuries. However, until now a satisfactory conventional explanation is not founded. At present above 2000 papers and reports have been published, above 200 various BL theories, linking BL to a variety of physical, chemical and nuclear processes, have been suggested. But none of these theories seems to have gained general acceptance because they fail to explain all observed characteristics of the phenomenon. A regular appearance of new theories confirms this conclusion and new theories are not exceptions. Systematization and classification of theories have been carried out. However, neither of them even approximately can explain enigmatic and intriguing BL behavior, which in a certain degree reminds the behavior of some highly organized matter. Physicists cannot imagine the object, submitting conventional physical laws, property of which coincides with BL properties. Explanation of Ball Lightning physics is deadlocked.

As was noted by Sagan [Sagan 2004], authors of the last book about Ball Lightning entitled "Ball Lightning: Paradox of Physics." All theories have one thing in common - none work. "Ball Lightning: an unsolved problem of Atmospheric Physics" - is the name of the monograph, published in 1999 [Stenhoff 1999]. We can specify this statement and say that the ball lightning is a shame of modern physics. It had penetrated the mysteries of a nuclear and the universe, knows when and how it originated, invented lasers and transistors, which have radically changed the conditions of life and human activity. However, the phenomenon of ball lightning, which is observed for centuries without any scientific instruments by thousands of observers, remains unexplained to this day.

Physicists cannot imagine an object obeying accepted laws of physics, the properties of which would coincide with the properties of ball lightning. Indeed, it is impossible to imagine an autonomous object that feels and bypasses obstacles penetrating into the premises through the windowpanes and the narrow slot while changing its shape. It can move against the wind, can accompany a flying plane in spite of the airflow speed that is greater than that in the strongest hurricane. It may even penetrate into the cabin and endanger the lives of passengers. Moreover, it emits a white light, like a body heated to several thousand degrees Celsius and at the same time, it does not burn. It is something completely new that is different from conventional material objects.

Just a twenty years ago, some scientists doubted that ball lightning even existed. But this is changing. Even the famous skeptics' association, the Committee for the Scientific Investigation of Claims of the Paranormal states on its Web site that ball lightning does indeed exist—but is unexplainable. Currently, there are numerous databases, which collected more than 10,000 eyewitness accounts, so there is no doubt that the BL exists.

A number of eminent physicists, for example, Calvin believed that this is nothing more than an optical illusion. Faraday was less categorical, however, and he believed that the BL is not associated with electrical phenomena (as follows from our book, he was right). In 1838, French scientist Arago published the first survey of twenty reports of ball lightning. After sixteen years of investigation, he wrote in 1854 "The Ball Lightnings of which I have cited so many examples, and which are so remarkable, first for the slowness and uncertainty of their movements, and next for the extent of the damage which they cause in exploding, appear to me to be one of the most inexplicable problems of physics today. These balls or globes of fire seem to be agglomerations of ponderable substances, strongly impregnated with the matter of lightning. How are such agglomerations formed? In what region do they originate? Whence are delivered the substances of which they are composed? What is their nature? Why do they sometimes pause for some time in their course, and afterward they rash off with great rapidity? In the face of these questions, science remains silent". At present once 176 years have been passed, scientists can answer no one of the put questions at this time. Moreover, the prospect of a solution of BL nature is foggiest, if new ideas will not be offered. It is extremely difficult to propose them because all conceivable hypotheses are already proposed, considered and recognized inconsistent.

Currently, science cannot answer any of the questions posed. Moreover, the prospects for resolution of this phenomenon is very vague. The study of the physics of ball lightning stalled. For example, a well-known journal Nature, which in the last century has published dozens of hypotheses, recently ceased publication of ball lightning with the desperation. Some fundamental new ideas are necessary. This is a very difficult task, because for centuries has been offered every conceivable hypothesis. However, none of them could explain the observed properties of ball lightning.

There are many different theories about the nature of the BL. Links to these can be found on the Internet by keyword "fireball" or «ball lightning». However, none of them is not universally accepted, as it cannot explain the many puzzling properties of BL.

Observational properties of BL are given in the book Stakhanov, who described in detail above hundred the most revealing events that he received from more than a thousand eyewitnesses. Sagan presented in his book [Sagan 2004] 230 unpublished cases from Top secret report of USA Oak Ridge National Laboratories in a systematic form. In his opinion, ball lightning violates known physics and "defies" gravity by its mysterious propulsion, navigation, confinement and quasi (as if) intelligent behavior. Even Nobel Prize winner such as Oppenheimer knew of its existence and were puzzled. Many theories begin by making restrictions and assumptions on boundary conditions that are untrue. But all theories ignore certain qualities, such as propulsion.

Properties of Ball lightning defy conventional physical interpretation, which leaves physicists shaking their heads in amazement and frustration. As a result of these contradictions, physicists respond to ball lightning in one of the several ways. Some avoid it; others deny it. Those who accept it attempt to explain it. This is impossible. The qualities are too contradictory and seem to violate physics. So they ignore or deny unexplainable qualities and selectively accept only those properties that physics might explain. These theories are respectable. Some get published. Since then, as the Sagan book was published, ten years have passed. The situation has not changed.

In accordance with Wikipedia, a review of the available literature published in 1972 identified the properties of a "typical" ball lightning, whilst cautioning against over-reliance on eyewitness accounts:

- BLs frequently appear almost simultaneously with cloud-to-ground lightning discharge
- BLs are generally spherical or pear-shaped with fuzzy edges
- BL diameters range from 1–100 cm, most commonly 10–20 cm
- BL brightness corresponds to roughly that of a domestic lamp, so they can be seen clearly in daylight
- A wide range of colors has been observed, red, orange, and yellow being the most common.
- The lifetime of each event is from 1 second to over a minute with the brightness remaining fairly constant during that time
- BLs tend to move, most often in a horizontal direction at a few meters per second, but may also move vertically, remain stationary or wander erratically.
- Many BLs are described as having rotational motion
- It is rare that observers report the sensation of heat, although in some cases the disappearance of the ball is accompanied by the liberation of heat
- Some BLs display an affinity for metal objects and may move along conductors such as wires or metal fences
- Some BLs appear within buildings passing through closed doors and windows
- Some BLs have appeared within metal aircraft and have entered and left without causing damage

- The disappearance of a BL is generally rapid and may be either silent or explosive
- Odors resembling ozone burning sulfur, or nitrogen oxides are often reported.

We will not comment these properties. The reader is referred to the systematization of the BL anomalous properties to the Sagan book [Sagan 2004]. The same book contains a list of the physical laws that are violated by BL in the Sagan opinion. In our opinion, no laws violate. Because of this to list these alleged violations is senseless. It makes sense to present the well-known laws of optics that govern the BL. Behavior.

A criterion that enables to evaluate various hypotheses is very simple. Really, since BL can penetrate through glass, BL should consist of substances that can penetrate through glass. Such substance cannot consist of particles because any particles (electrons, ions, atoms, molecules, clusters, motes, etc.) cannot penetrate through glass. We can conclude that BL has no weight because only particles are ponderable. The same conclusion can be derived from the fact that BL can move against the wind. Not have to be a prominent physicist to understand that any particles should be blown away by wind independently on inner processes within BL. According to this criterion, almost all existing hypotheses should be rejected. The exception is not provided by the most popular at the present day BL theory of Abrahamson and Dennis. They propose that the BL exists due to oxidation of silicon nano-particles in the atmosphere. The silicon nano-particlesare formed as a result of a reaction of silicon oxides and carbon in the soil during a lightning strike. Common sense suggests that these particles are carried away by the airstream and cannot penetrate through the glass window.

An exception is made only for hypotheses in which the occurrence of BL is connected with the presence of external fields and BL represents some discharge in the place where the concentration of these fields takes place. However, these hypotheses failed to explain BL behavior that is determined by the objects surrounding it rather than hypothetical external fields. For example, the BL penetrates into the space through the slot, modifying its shape in such a way that it could leak through the slot. BL penetrates into the room through the glass pane, rather than instead of through the wall. BL avoids obstacles in the room. BL is moving around the floor, rather than near the ceiling.

If the BL cannot consist of particles, it is unclear from what else it could be. It may consist of light because it emits light. Light can penetrate through the windows. The glass panes are designed to penetrate the light through them. The light beam is not blown away by the wind. However, as is well known, light travels in straight lines. Usually, the light beam is cited as an example a straight line. Generally speaking, the light beam can be bent in the direction of increasing the refractive index of the atmosphere in which it is propagating, rather than in the direction of the wind. This explains the mirage in the desert. However, the radius of curvature of the light beam is tens of kilometers. Speed of light is extremely great. Because of this, light is indifferent to the speed at which an object moves. For example, the speed of the airplane is smaller than that of light by a factor of one million.

What is Ball Lightning?

In 2002 we put forward the hypothesis that the Ball Lightning is a self-confined light. The Ball Lightning can be imagined as the soap bubble where the soap film is replaced by the film of strongly compressed air. The conventional white light is circulating in the film in all possible directions. The film shows itself as a planar wave guide the curvature of which is different from zero. The wave guide prevents the radiation of the light in free space. In turn, the light compresses the air due to the electrostriction pressure. This combination is closer to the light rather than to the lightning. We cut the tail in the world lightning and will call this combination by Ball Light.

We have shown that the energy of the light is essentially greater than that on the compressed air. In this case the behavior of the Ball Light is determined by the forces connected with the light rather than by the conventional forces connected with material particles. Said forces were considered in numerous hypotheses but all attempts to explain the mysterious behavior of the Ball Lightning failed.

On the contrary, we have succeeded to explain all features of the Ball Lightning behavior on assumption that the forces between the light and matter play a decisive role. Our theory is mentioned in Wikipedia.

Explanation of the Ball Lightning nature is much simpler than you can expect. Ball Lightning is a combination of the conventional atmosphere air and the conventional white light radiated at a strike of the usual Lightning. This is a spherical thin film of the strongly compressed air where the intensive white light circulates in all possible directions. If you imagine a soap bubble where the soap film is replaced with the compressed air and rotating light, you obtain Ball Lightning. In fact, this is a Ball Light. From now on we will cut the tail in the word Lightning and will use the term Ball Light. The air pressure inside the soap bubble volume is greater than that outside. On the contrary, these pressures in the Ball Light are identical. This provides its great deformability.

The refractive index of the compressed air in the film is increased. Then the film shows itself as a planar light guide the curvature of which differs from zero. The lightguide prevents radiation of the light in free space. In turn, the circulating light produces the electrostriction pressure that provides the compression of the air.

A local minimum of the total energy of the air and the light takes place. As a result, this combination is stable. The light energy stored in the Ball Light is decreasing gradually because of its glow. The air pressure and the refractive index decreases also. Below some threshold Ball Light becomes instable. The light radiates in all directions of free space. The compressed air expands. The Ball Light disappears without a trace.

The energy of the light is significantly greater than the energy of the compressed air. As a result, a behavior of the Ball Light is determined by the light rather than the air. The light is subject to action of perfectly different optically induced forces. In the same time the light does not obey the laws of gravity.

Of course, the assumption that there are Ball Lights in the nature is quite unusual. Nobody previously suspected about an existence of Ball Lights. Therefore, Ball Lights could not been studied either theoretically or experimentally. Moreover, there are not even a single mention. The authors initially believed that these objects could only be the fruit of unbridled imagination, or inflammation, or mockery of physicists. However, a priori assuming incredible that such objects exist, authors found to his great amazement that the behavior of these objects in the Earth's atmosphere according to the known laws of physics completely coincides with a mysterious and intriguing behavior of ball lightning.

The question arises. What is advantage of the presented theory over other known above 200 theories? The answer is simple. Our theory explains Ball Lightning properties that can not explain other theories. The most demonstrative puzzles are the following

1.   Horizontal motion at constant speed near the surface of the ground at distance about 1 meter.

2.   Penetration in rooms through window panes. Any objects consisting of particles (molecules ions, electrons and so on) can not penetrate but the light can.

3.   Penetration through gaps

4.   Catching up flying aircrafts.

To explain these puzzles we need to take into account the following simple physical facts.

BL is the extremely sensitive device that senses the smallest change of the density of the surrounding air. BL moves along the gradient of the air density.

The air density depends on the temperature. The greater the temperature, the smaller density. Then BL moves against the gradient of the temperature.

If the gradient of the air density is constant at the distance of BL diameter, BL shape is spherical. Otherwise, various parts of BL surface move differently and BL shape is deformed. This situation takes place when BL is located near any obstacle. BL heats up the obstacle. The obstacle heats up the nearby air and the gradient of the air density is changed in the local region.

Laws of optics for explanation of the paradoxes

Unlike the propagation of light in free space where light beams are propagating in a straight line, the propagation of light in an optical medium is determined by its refractive index n that can be various in various regions of space. Laws of propagation of light in the optical medium are known since time of Newton. The first of them is the Snell law that determined a relation between angles of incidence θ_1 and transmission θ_2 at the incidence of a light beam at a plane boundary between two optical medium with the refractive indexes n_1 and n_2, respectively (see Fig. 1a). The relation between angles is given by

$$Sin\theta_1/Sin\theta_2 = n_2/n_1 \qquad (1)$$

As is seen, the light beam is deflected in the side of the optical medium refractive index of which is greater. If we have several boundaries between optical mediums as is shown in Fig.1b, the angle of transmission is decreasing at each transmission. In a limiting case when the refractive index is changed continuously along the z axis, we obtain that the angle of the transmission is

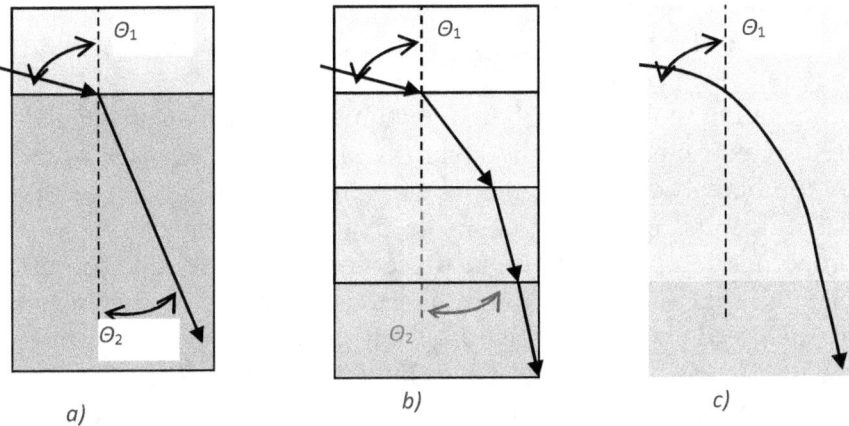

a)   b)   c)

Fig. 1. Propagation of light in inhomogeneous optical mediums.
a) through the boundary of two medium where the refractive index of lower one is greater than that of the upper one.
b) through the boundary of four mediums where the refractive index of lower one is greater than that of the upper one.
c) through the boundary of the medium the refractive index of which increases gradually

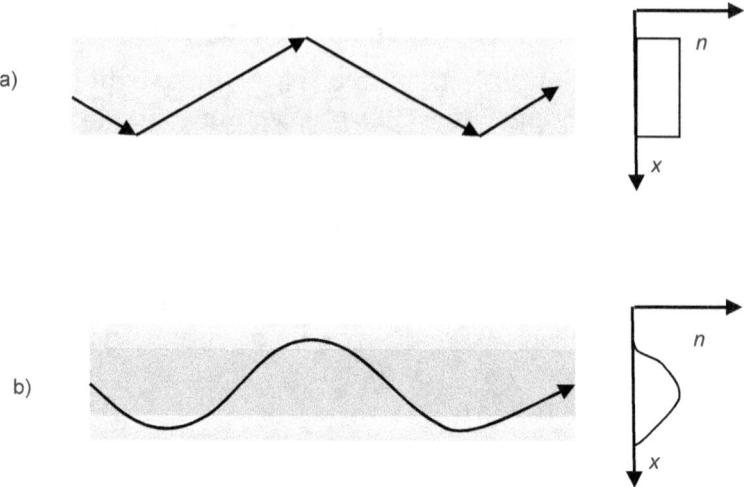

Fig. 2. Trajectories of the light beam in inhomogeneous mediums.
c) sharps boundaries between the waveguide and free space.
d) A gradual change of the refractive index along the width of the waveguide
Dependencies of the refractive index on the width of the waveguide are shown at the right hand.

changed continuously as is shown in Fig.1c.

In accordance with the Snell law, there is the phenomenon of the total inner reflection if $n_2/n_1>1$. Then the light beam propagating in the layer of an optical medium that is surrounded by free space cannot leave the layer (see Fig. 2a). The layer is called by the planar waveguide that is used in the wide section of optics named by the integral optics. The planar waveguide preserves its properties to confine the light if the boundary between the optical medium and free space is not sharp as is shown in Fig.2a but is gradual as is shown in Fig. 2b. The planar waveguides preserve their property to confine the light if their curvature is different from zero (see Fig.3a). In particular, the curve planar waveguide can be closed (see Fig. 3b). In this case, the wave is circulated around the axis of the cylinder. Such waves are called by the whispering gallery waves (WGW). In other particular case, the planar waveguide can be closed in two mutually perpendicular directions as is shown in Fig 3c. In this case, we obtain the spherical layer where WGW can propagate in all possible directions.

Let us now consider propagation of the same wave in the same optical mediums but their refractive index depends on the intensity of the light wave. Usually, the refractive index increases with an increase of the intensity. The conventional air of the terrestrial atmosphere is the nonlinear optical medium also. Its refractive index increases with an increase of the intensity because the intensive light compresses the air. Its density increases and, therefore, the refractive index increases because the greater density, the greater the refractive index. It is known since 1975 that the plane light of finite width w produces in a homogeneous nonlinear optical medium the region where the refractive index is increased. In this case, we have the same planar waveguide as is shown in Fig. 2b. The combination of the light and the planar waveguide formed by the light is called by the space optical planar solition. Properties of such solitons are well studied. It is shown that they can confine the light like conventional planar waveguide where refractive index is independent of the intensity.

Having performed the same procedure as shown in figure 3, we obtain that the spherical space soliton (SSS) can be imagined. Unlike the space optical planar solution, properties of SSS have

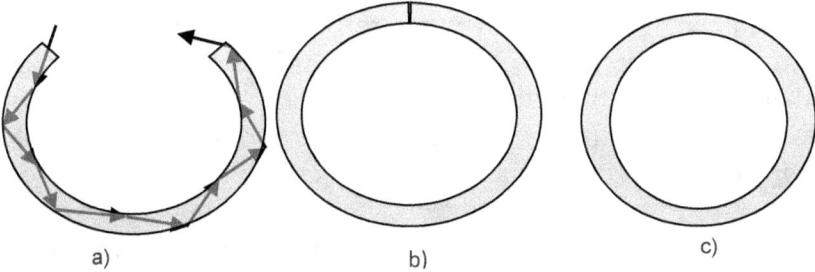

a)   b)   c)

Fig.3. Types of curved planar waveguides
a) Partially curved waveguide
b) closed planar waveguide curved in one direction that forms the cylindrical layer where light wave can circulate.
c) Closed planar waveguide curved in two mutually perpendicular directions that forms the spherical layer where light wave can propagate in all possible directions. Fig.2. Propagation of light in planar waveguides
Trajectories of the light beam in inhomogeneous mediums.
a)   sharps boundaries between the waveguide and free space.
b)   A gradual change of the refractive index along the width of the waveguide
Dependencies of the refractive index on the width of the waveguide are shown at the right hand.

never been studied. Moreover, nobody suspected about a possibility of the SSS existence. Really, it is hard to imagine that the conventional white light, that propagates in a straight line, can be confined in the volume about one liter and no additional objects besides the conventional air is required for this purpose. SSS cannot be imagined at present day by the scientific community. That is why it is believed that the enigma of the Ball Lightning has not been resolved yet.

Many physicists, who believe that they are prominent ones, cannot imagine that the conventional air the reflection index of which differs from 1 by $2.7 \cdot 10^{-4}$ can confine the light in the volume about one liter. They cannot imagine that a small change of the refractive index can force the light to rotate along the trajectory that radius is about 5 cm. Now we will not prove that the prominent physicists are wrong. We will give the following simple unambiguous example to overcome their misconception.

As is known the optical single mode fiber used in the telecommunication consists of the glass core of about 10 μm diameter and glass coating of 125 μm diameter. The refractive index of the core is greater than that of the coating by about one percent or smaller. The light propagates inside the core due to the phenomenon of the total inner reflection. Like the curve planar waveguide, the curve optical fiber confines the light. It turns out that the confinement takes place even in the case when the fiber is wound on the finger. In this case, the radius of the curvature is smaller than 1 cm. To provide an increase of the refractive index of the air by one percent, the air should be compressed by about 40 times at the pressure about 40 atmospheres. There are observations that testify that BL ceases its existence with the sound that reminds the pistol shot. The pressure of gasses in the barrel of the pistol is significantly greater. Further, we will show that there is a majority of other means to increase the refractive index in the SSS shell.

Now we need to show that the SSS tends to move in the direction where the refractive index is increasing. The rigorous proof by means of the quantitative analysis of optically induced force applied to the SSS from the side of the air will be given in the theoretical chapter. Now it is sufficient to use the above-mentioned property of light to bend in the direction where the refractive index is decreasing to a maximal degree. As is known from mathematics, this direction is determined by the gradient of the refractive index.

The next obvious physical law is the following.

1. The air refractive index is increasing with the air density. The air refractive index is equal to 1 when the air density is equal to 0. The air refractive index is equal to $1+\Delta n$ where $\Delta n=0.00027$ at normal condition when the air pressure is equal 100 000 Pa and the air density is equal to 1.4 kg/m3. The SSS moves in the direction of the gradient of the air density.

2. The air density is in inverse proportion with the air temperature at the constant air pressure. In this case, the gradient of the air temperature is opposite to the gradient of the air density. We can say that SSS moves opposite to the gradient of the air temperature.

3. The air density is in direct proportion with the air temperature at the constant air temperature. In this case, the gradient of the air pressure is parallel to the gradient of the air density. We can say that SSS moves along the gradient of the air pressure.

4. Directions of the air velocity and the air acceleration in the conventional air atmosphere can be different. This means that directions of the wind and the gradient of the air pressure can be different. Since SSS moves along the gradient of the air pressure rather that the along the direction of the wind, direction of the SSS motion and wind can be different.

It turns out that this elementary information is sufficient to explain all listed above paradoxes.

The answers to the riddles

Overcoming Gravity

Bearing in mind that Ball Lightning (BL) is a ball light (Ball Light) let us consider the behavior of the Ball Light in the air atmosphere. Motionless Ball Light in a homogeneous atmosphere remains stationary. Indeed, in this case, there is a central symmetry in the system, and there is the chosen direction.

If the Ball Light is located in an inhomogeneous medium, the refractive index n of which depends on the spatial coordinates, the situation changes. A light beam propagating in an inhomogeneous optical medium is deflected in the direction of the gradient of the refractive index. Then we can conclude that any closed beam circulating in the Ball Light shell is deflected in the direction of the gradient of the refractive index of the atmosphere in which it is located. In other words, Ball Light moves to the direction where the air density is increasing.

BL is a sensitive instrument for determining the inhomogeneity of the air density (provided that the composition of the air at all points of space is the same). Indeed, if we imagine that the light that is circulating in the Ball Light shifts by 1 micrometer only per one revolution, then a shift is equal to 1 km per one second. This is due to the very high velocity of light $3 \ 10^8$ m/s. For example, if the Ball Light circumferential length is equal to 30 cm, the light makes every second one billion revolutions. Billion shifts of one micrometer give the shift of 1 km.

Existing theories cannot explain the simplest things. For what reasons BLs are moving in the atmosphere as they move? For example, Turner [Turner 1998] is puzzling that the BLs falling to the ground from the clouds, often stop before hitting the earth's surface. Moreover, Sagan came to the conclusion that the BL is not subject to gravity and presented the theory of Everything, Defining the gravity because he cannot explain this fact in the framework of the existing physical ideas,.

Our explanation for this phenomenon is quite simple and natural. Ball Light is heavier than air because compressed air in the shell is heavier than air at atmospheric pressure that surrounds the shell. Ball Light fells to the ground like a normal child's balloon because the net force of the gravity and Archimedesforceis directed toward the ground. However, there is another type of force that has never been anywhere considered in the framework of the BL studies. This is optically induced force. We spent a few years (2012 -2014) to show that existing approaches to the analysis and calculation of the optically induced forces (OIF) are erroneous [Torchigin 2012-2014]. We have shown that the Lorentz force approach, that has been used for the last 40 years, is incorrect because it gives an incorrect result in the simplest case. [Torchigin 2014 Phys. Rev.] Besides, we have presented a resolution to the age-old problem of the theoretical physics known as the Abraham-Minkowski dilemma about a magnitude of the momentum of light in matter [Torchigin 2014 Physics Research international]. We have also shown that the propagation of a light pulse in matteris is accompanied by pressures arising in the regions where the leading and trailing edges of the pulse are propagating. In this connection, it is not surprising that our optical theory of ball lightning has not wined a generally accepted recognition yet. Further success in the recognition is connected directly with a correct notion of the scientific community about the nature of optically induced forces and their properties.

It is believed that optically induced forces are extremely small because significant efforts are required for their experimental observation. It is valid for the conventional intensity of light. But the intensity of light in the Ball Light shell is increased by billion times. Indeed, the intensity is defined as the energy that passes through a square of unit area per unit time. Since the same light crosses the cross-section of the shell billion times per second, the intensity inside the shell is increased by billion times as compared with the intensity of the same light beam propagating recliner that crosses the cross-section of the square only one time. In this case,the magnitude of the optically induced force applied to Ball Light is sufficient to exert a decisive influence on the behavior of BL in the earth's atmosphere.

The optically induced force, that acts on an inhomogeneous optical medium on the side of circulating light in BL shell,is directed in the direction opposite to the gradient of the refractive index of the medium.This means that there is a force in accordance with the third Newton law that acts on the light on the side of the optical medium (on the side of surrounding the air). The force is directed along the gradient of the surrounding air. Since the circulating light cannot leave the BL shell, the force is applied to the Ball Light shell. Similar situation takes place for the force applied to a conductor with electrical current located in a magnetic field. In accordance with the Ampere law, there is the force applied to the conductor. In reality, the force is applied to electrons moving within the conductor. Since the electrons cannot leave the conductor and go out into free space, the force is redistributed to the conductor. Thus, there is optically induced force in an inhomogeneous air that is directed along the gradient of the air refractive index.

As the air pressure decreases with increasing altitude, the air density also decreases and hence the gradient of the refractive index is directed downwards. Since Ball Light moves along the gradient of the refractive index, Ball Light falls down until the gradient of the refractive index is directed downwards. But Ball Light does not reach the earth's surface. The reason is that immediately at the earth's surface temperature is greater than that at the height of several meters.This is due to heating the surface of the earth by solar radiation. As a result, there is a maximum of the air density at a certain distance from the surface. At this altitude, Ball Light stops its movement in the vertical direction. The force of gravity acting on the Ball Light is not essential since the optically induced forces exceed the force of gravity. More accurate to say that the Ball Light is located below the maximum of the refractive index where the optically induced force (OIF) directed upwards is equal to the force of gravity directed downwards. Stopping the vertical movement, Ball Light continues to move in the horizontal direction along the horizontal component of the gradient of the refractive index at the height where the vertical component of the gradient of the refractive index is equal to zero. That is why the observed BL is mainly moving at low height in the horizontal direction.

We can remind to the reader that the fog lamps on vehicles are located as close as possible to the surface of the earth because the air near the surface has the maximal temperature, and the mist at the temperature is not formed. Therefore, the fog lamp shines the road to a greater distance. The air refractive index decreases with increasing temperature and, therefore, there is a maximum of the refractive index at a certain height from the earth' surface where Ball Light is moving. Thus, the intriguing behavior of BL, giving the appearance that the Ball Light does not obey the laws of gravity, is explained naturally if the optically induced forces are taken into consideration.

Uniform horizontal movement

Note that the usual children's balloon cannot move by inertia in the horizontal direction for a long time, since the initial horizontal component of velocity decreases rapidly to zero due to the Stokes force. Stokes force is responsible for the resistance experienced from the air by any moving body. As a result, the pressure on the front hemisphere of BL is greater than that on the back hemisphere. Then the refractive index near the front hemisphere is greater than that near the back hemisphere. Since BL tends to move in the direction where the refractive index increases, there is an optically induced force directed opposite to the Stokes force. This force can compensate the Stokes force and BL can move horizontally as if the Stokes force is absent.

Explanation bouncing

There are BLs the net force of the weight and the Archimedes force of which is directed downwards and surpasses the optically induced force. In this case BL tends towards the surface of the ground. At a small distance from the surface of the earth, BL heats this surface due to its light radiation. As a result, the temperature of the air in the gap between BL and the surface increases significantly, and a great gradient of the temperature directed towards the surface rises. Therefore, there is a great gradient of the refractive index directed upwards that increases gradually as BL approaches the ground. This gradient is responsible for a rise of OIF directed upwards. The vertical velocity of the BL directed towards the ground decreases gradually, becomes equal to zero, and then increases in the opposite direction. BL bounces off the ground and moves upwards. As the distance between BL and the ground increase, the gradient of the refractive index is decreased, and optically induced force is also decreased. As a result, there is a time instant when the net force of the gravity and Archimedes force begins to surpass the optically induced forces and BL begins to move with the acceleration directed downwards. The vertical velocity becomes equal to zero at a certain height and BL begins to move downwards. Ball Light is ready for the next jump. A similar situation occurs with a stone thrown vertically upwards.

The same result we obtain if there is some latency in heating. For example, the floor is wet, and a certain time is required for its heating. Ball Light approaches a wet floor at the distance that is smaller than that for a dry floor because the feedback comes into play with some delay. In this case, the air temperature between Ball Light and the wet floor is greater, and Ball Light repels from the floor. The amplitude of Ball Light oscillations depends on the degree of floor wetness. Since the refractive index of the water vapors at normal pressure is equal to nwater=1.0002354 and the refractive index of the air at normal pressure is equal to nair=1.0002727, then the refractive index of appearing gas mixture decreases not only owning increase in the temperature but also owning insertion in the air the gas component with smaller refractive index. Thus, a wet obstacle promotes better repulsion from it.

Bypassing obstacles

Moving horizontally Ball Light itself may also change the temperature distribution, and thus the air density and the refractive index around itself, particularly when approaching obstacles. With the same air pressure, the air density is inversely proportional to temperature, so Ball Light moves in a direction opposite the temperature gradient. Approaching some obstacles, Ball Light heats it by means of the emitted radiation. In turn, the obstacle heats the surrounding air due to the phenomenon of heat conduction and thus decreases its refractive index. There is the gradient of the refractive index directed from the obstacle. Moving along this gradient, Ball Light bounce off the obstacle or bypasses it. Outwardly, it looks as if the Ball Light "feels" the obstacle and avoids it.

Why directions of the wind and a motion of the ball lightning can be different

Another clue to the anomalous properties of the Ball Light is associated with an explanation of why the direction of motion of the Ball Light may not coincide with the direction of the wind. As is marked by Sagan [Sagan 2014], Ball Light flying against a breeze or the wind is commonly reported. Why and how? Flying against the wind takes energy. For a fireball without any apparent means of propulsion, this is a mystery and was why scientists doubted ball lightning. According to existing physics, there is no explanation at all for how fireballs can fly, let alone against the wind.

Sagan presents the following observations.

It was 9:30 a.m. during a severe June storm in 1963. I am an engineer, an MIT graduate, and a licensed pilot. I now live in Massachusetts, but in 1963 was living on Phoenix Drive in Fort Worth, Texas. The house stood in the residential section but had adjoining fields. We stood at the East window watching the hailstorm. A severe June storm struck at 9:30 am. It was a frontal storm, with an alleged tornado that turned over trucks half a mile away, blowing out car windows and damaging our house. Noise was intense. I did not see the fireball materialize, the rain and hail were intense, and we could see little-just a bright-but-not-dazzling white fireball. I think it would have been dazzling in the absence of the storm. At first, I thought a power line blew down. The fireball was near a cotton wood tree. After the storm, I went out and found no damage. Then I realized that the fireball's drift had been to the south, against the wind. Although I cannot say for certain,it was a sphere; it seemed two feet in diameter. We were 30 feet away from it. It fell to the ground from fifty feet up at a falling speed of 20 miles per hour in a curved path, flying against an intense wind. I have heard eyewitnesses describe ball lightning rolling in the Colorado mountains.

This is another observation. The Rain was imminent. To the right of a military jeep in a convoy, a bright orange ten-inch fireball the color of a sodium lamp appeared between an opening in the wire fence and then floated parallel to the jeep, staying twenty feet from it, about five feet above the ground flying at thirty miles per hour. It glided deliberately despite a fierce wind and vanished after fifteen seconds.

Stanley Singer in case 171, on page43, of Ball Lightning, reported a case in 1949 from the West German encounter. Despite a power fulgale, a dazzling white fireball floated in the air ten feet above the ground and 40 feet from the house. The size of a full moon, it emitted rays. The ball broke up, leaving a glowing crescent, like a new moon, but curved down-ward. A vibrant discharge shot to the ground and a spark in the air. Still floating at ten feet in the air and impervious to the gale wind, the original fireball or its remnant emitted many one-foot red-yellow sparks. This phase lasted four seconds. A fist-sized glowing mass hit the earth and sprayed out red sparks.

The explanation is quite simple. Ball Light moves along the gradient of the refractive index, the direction of which may not coincide with the direction of the air velocity. This short and simple explanation is sufficient. However, it makes sense to give some comments.

Fig. 4 presents a special case of an air vortex. In this case, the velocity of air is directed tangentially to the circumference. The air pressure is identical on the circle due the axial symmetry. Then the tangential component of the pressure gradient is zero, and the pressure gradient is directed along the radius. When approaching the center, the pressure decreases. It provides the appearance of centripetal forces propelling the air masses with the centripetal acceleration directed toward the center of the circle. Since the refractive index is proportional to the pressure, the gradient of the refractive index is perpendicular to the velocity of air and in this case. Ball Light moves perpendicularly to the wind.

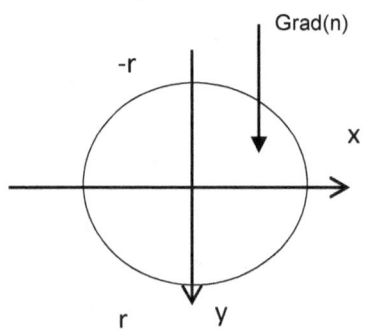

Fig.4. Direction of coordinate axis relatively the infinite cylindrical layer

Note that if the air is moving through a tube or slit, the

24

pressure gradient is directed in the direction opposite the movement. In this case, unlike all the known movement of objects that moves in the direction of the air, Ball Light moves oppositely to air. This property provides Ball Light penetration into the cabin of aircrafts through the splits and holes through which the air inside the cabin goes.

The same property is used in the hypothesis that the reason of the Chernobyl tragedy was BL, occurring when the experiment began with switching large currents. BL penetrated into the steam line and started moving in a direction against the movement of steam, i.e. in the direction towards the active zone where the steam pressure is maximal. BL brought the reactor from normal mode, and the reactor exploded in a few tens of seconds [Torchigin 2006 bulletin on atomic energy].

Why ball lightning seems cold

One additional argument in favor of the optical nature of BL is the explanation of the following apparent contradiction. Most physicists, if not all, wonder why BL emits white light, the spectrum of which corresponds to the temperature of the hot glowing body of several thousand degrees, and at the same time BL is relatively cold, as it does not burn the objects around it. This paradox has a simple explanation.

A light that emits Ball Light is not the light that radiates a scorching body. The light radiated by Ball Light is the light arising due to the molecular light scattering of the intense light circulating in the Ball Light shell. Indeed, the white light was generated by excited atoms of the air heated to a high temperature during the gas discharge of a linear lightning in which the BL appeared. This light was caught in a bubble of light, and there exists a relatively long time. Ball Light may already be far from its place of origin, and the air in the Ball Light at this time may already become cool.Thus, the nature of the light radiated by Ball Light differs from the nature of light radiated by a hot body. Ball Light caught and canned a light radiation of a conventional linear lightning strike, and gradually radiated it in the form of scattered light.

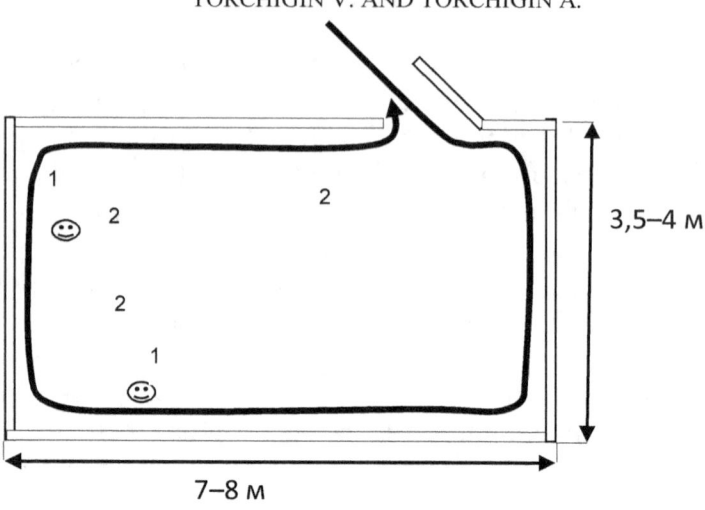

Рис. 5. Trace of the BL motion in the shed of builders. 1 – observers; 2 – tables.

Explanation of circles inside perimeter

Sagan devotes an entire section describing the motion of BL on the perimeter of the room. There are some of these cases.

Lightning struck a tree several hundred feet away, and a six-inch ball flashed across and into the open end of a garage, followed the wall counterclockwise around the garage on the floor or the ground level. It faded as it left the garage.

Orange ball circles radio transmitter room. Lightning struck a radio transmitter antenna. I was in the transmitter room. Transmitter equipment was destroyed and melted. The fireball was not a flash, but an orange flame sphere that traveled quickly about the room leaving an ozone odor.

Garage blue ball floats back and forth. After an earlier storm in early June, in the weather hot and humid, just before sunset, a man walked into his garage. A basketball-sized blue fireball with a large electrical coating floated on the left side, floated right, and then back to the left like a caged animal, then vanished. The garage was dark, and the doors were closed. Was the ball there before he opened the door? Was the ball trying to escape?

26

Stakhanov [Stakhanov 1996] in the case of number 29 describes the motion of the BL in a closed trajectory in the trailer where builders lived. The trace of the BL in the shed is shown in Fig. 5. As expected, the BL, approaching next wall, changes its direction of motion, and starts to move along the wall again.

Typically, walls are cooler than the air in the middle of the premises because the walls are connected to the ground that is cooler than the surrounding air. If the room has a stove, it heats first the air around him, and then the air is heated wall. Walls alter the above-described linear motion of Ball Light with constant velocity as follows. Approaching the wall, Ball Light heats the wall due to Ball Light radiation. The wall heats the adjacent air. The gradient of the refractive index of the air is directed away from the wall. As a result, the movement of the Ball Light towards wall stops and the Ball Light moves along the wall. Since the air before Ball Light is colder than rear, Ball Light continues to move along the walls at a distance from them. In some cases, the Ball Light is approaching the door. If Ball Light heated indoor air to such an extent that the air outside is colder than outside, the Ball Light leaves the premises.

Explanation of the ball lightning motion in a room near a floor rather than near ceiling

It is easy to explain the features of the BL motion indoors. As is known, the air inside the room is closer to a steady state than outside. Since warm air is lighter than cold air, the air near the floor cooler than the air near the ceiling, and hence the refractive index of the air is the maximum near the floor. In this case, has penetrated into the room, BL moves toward the floor, which in this case acts as an obstacle. There are many reports that BL, penetrated into the room, moving around the floor. In some cases, the motion is accompanied by bouncing. The explanation is given below.

Explanation how the ball lightning finds out splits, holes, and chimneys to penetrate through them

Before considering the mechanisms that ensure the penetration of BL through small cracks and openings, let us answer a simple question - how BL finds out similar objects. Actually, why not BL indifferent to the cracks and holes. It is clear that the BL has no organs of sight, smell, touch, that are in living beings. However, BL can "feel" the slightest change in the refractive index of the environment and move along the gradient of the refractive index. We show that the splits and holes are sources of such changes

Consider the motion of BL near the tunnel between a room and outside space. Suppose that the room temperature is lower than outside, and the air pressure inside and outside the same. In this case, the density of the air in the room is greater than that outside, and the gradient of the refractive index on the axis of the tunnel is directed into the room. Since the density of the air when moving along the tunnel varies gradually and continuously, the surfaces of equal density have the form shown in Fig. 6 solid lines. Dashed lines in the figure are perpendicular to these surfaces. The direction of the tangent to any such line at any point coincides with the direction of the gradient of the refractive index at that point. It is easy to verify that the BL, moving along any of the dashed lines from various points A, B, C, moves toward the tunnel. An original funnel is created near the tunnel. Caught in this funnel, BL fall into the tunnel

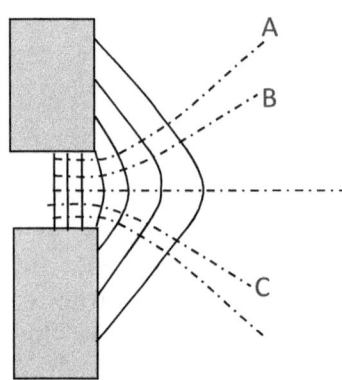

Fig. 6. Surfaces of equal temperatures and refractive indexes near the split in a wall are shown by solids. Tangents to the surface to the directions of the gradient of the refractive index are shown by dotted lines

Similarly, BL finds out roof chimneys to penetrate through them into the room. There is a funnel around each tube. Falling from a height, BL falls into one of these funnels and begins its movement along the gradient of the refractive index. If necessary, BL can change its shape as

28

was discussed above.

Explanation of penetration in rooms through small splits and holes

BL can penetrate into the room through the door cracks, windows, chimneys, may leave the premises. There are numerous reports that BL moved along the walls of the room at a certain height, avoiding the emerging obstacles in their way, comes to slots and penetrates through it into the room. The dimensions of the slots or openings can be considerably smaller than the diameter of the BL.

There is a huge amount of evidence that BL can penetrate through small slits. Let us present a few of them, taken from the book of Stakhanov [Stakhanov 1996].

During a severe thunderstorm, BL of 20-30 cm in diameter entered through a hole in the wall for grounding.

During thunderstorms, BL 10 cm in diameter penetrated in the hole 2 cm wide. BL deformed in "stretched sausage." while penetration.

BL 10-20 cm diameter went into the crack around the window glass.

BL diameter of 30-50 cm entered through a small hole in the window (glass chipped corner) 1-1.5 cm in width as the "yellow thread".Having done a few laps around the room, BL exploded after 20-30 seconds.

BL 5-10 cm in diameter entered as a "snake" during a thunderstorm through the open window and then forming a bead. After going around the room a distance of 5-10 m, BL disappeared without an explosion near the switch.

During a severe thunderstorm, BL entered the house in the gap between the boards around the pipe. The board was smoked. The fire began.

BL 10-20 cm in diameter passed through a hole diameter of 8 cm.

BL « the size of a tennis ball" has gone through a closed window, in which the glass had a crack.

BL «flowed" in the hole between the logs in the forge room. The slit width was much smaller than the BL diameter. BL was a ball with a diameter of 12-13 cm, orange, brightness of the lamp 50-100 watts.

Yellow ball the size of a large orange was creeping through the crack in the wall. Rather, it was not creeping but was poured from one-half to the other.

BL walked into the room through a hole in the glass, was flattened, as its size was larger than the hole. Eyewitnesses clarify: "the ball was in the 10-15 cm from our faces, and we have seen well as he began to pass through the hole, taking the form of a melon. He stretched out, was less in diameter and passed through the hole. When the ball passed through the hole and decreased in size, it was shaking all the time, and it seems that it consists of jelly".

Consider the reasons for which BL can change its shape to penetrate into the room through a small slit or hole. First, we must explain the reasons responsible for its spherical shape in a uniform air and its deformation in the no uniform air. As already mentioned, there is a sufficiently high air pressure in the BL shell. The spherical shape provides a minimum of compressed air energy amongst other possible shapes. However, this does not mean that BL is like toy balloons, which is difficult to deform significantly. The Air pressure exists only in a thin BL shell of several micrometers thickness. This pressure provides the spherical BL shape, but to a much lesser extent because small external forces can significantly change the BL shape. It reminds a shell of a baby balloon from which the air is removed, and the balloon is placed in a vacuum and weightlessness. The shell takes the form of a sphere under the action of its own weak elastic forces tending to straighten it and make it flat. Since the topology of the shell is such that it cannot be planar, the elastic forces in the absence of other forces result in that the shell takes the form of a ball. This shell can be easily stretched through a wedding ring. This cannot be done with a shell, which is filled with the air, like the children's balloons.

A similar situation holds for the BL shell, which adopts a spherical shape in a homogeneous optical medium due to the

CLUE OF BALL LIGHTNING PUZZLES

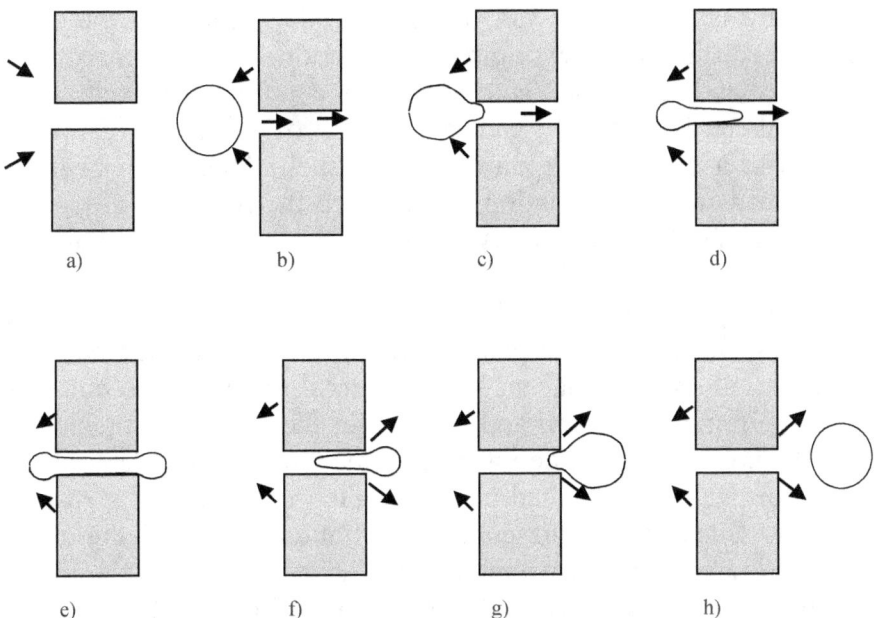

Fig.7. Sequential steps of penetration of the light ball through the split in a wall.

elastic properties of the layer of compressed air in the shell. The BL form can be easily changed in the same a way as the spherical shape of the elastic child balloon in vacuo is changed in the weightlessness.

When the BL is approaching the opening in the wall, wherein the gradient of refractive index of air is directed to the wall, a distribution of the gradient of the refractive index shown in Fig. 6 is changed due to the appearance of the next effect of self-action. When approaching the BL to the opening, inhomogeneous of air increases because BL heats the wall, which in turn heats the layer of the air between the BL and hole. Thus, BL indirectly heats the air. Solid objects, that absorb radiation radiated by BL, must first be heated. The regions surrounding the hole are used as these objects. These regions heat adjacent air layers due to the phenomenon of heat conduction.

The closer the air layer to the opaque surface of the wall, the higher its temperature. When heated, the density and the refractive index of the air decreases. Forces arise that repels BL regions,

31

which are closer to the wall, from the wall surface. At the same time, according to our original assumption the gradient of the refractive index directed into the room continues to exist. As a result, there is optically induced forces of different directions applied to a different region of the BL shell. The action of these forces leads to a deformation of BL since the reducing properties of the BL shell are extremely weak. BL takes the form shown in Figure 7c.

As BL penetrates into the hole, as shown in Figure 7d, the following feedback takes place. The shorter the distance between the BL shell and an adjacent lateral internal region of the hole, the more the region is heated and the greater the force of repulsion of the BL shell from the side internal surface of the hole. As a result, the deformed BL is located in the middle of the hole as shown in Fig. 7e. Subsequent phases of penetration BL into the room through the hole are shown in Figures 7f, 7g, 7h.

Thus, the forces associated with the initial gradient of the refractive index of air, "drags» BL through a hole in the wall. BL recovers its original spherical shape after it has passed the hole and hit the uniform indoor air. It is easy to see that the same physical effects are responsible both for BL penetration through a hole and for BL horizontal movement at a certain distance from the earth's surface. Since the thickness of the shell BL can be extremely thin, BL can penetrate through a very narrow gap of the tens of micrometer width.

Similar processes take place at Ball Light penetration into the cabin of the aircraft. As is known, the air pressure is small at high altitude where aircrafts fly. To provide the normal air pressure within the aircraft, outdoor air is pumped continuously. At the same time, the indoor air penetrates outdoor through any holes and slots. These are excellent places for BL to penetrate indoor. First, the air pressure in these places is greater than the air pressure in the vicinity. Second, the gradient of the air pressure is directed inwards because the indoor pressure is greater than the outdoor one.

The following an incident, that occurred in the Vologda region in February 1946, is rather indicative. Copilot saw that the bright white ball appeared on the right wing of the aircraft near the running green lamp. He thought that it was a short-circuit bulb, but the flash will not disappear, as usually happens. The ball slowly crawled along the front edge of the wing, and disappeared under the nose of the airplane, there was a loud crack, and the black smoke threw in the pilot, the connection was lost.

The commander asked the navigator, "Nicholas, maybe you noticed how the ball rolled out? After all, he appeared right at your feet. "The navigator replied, "I took the pistol to check the color in her charge. But I do not have time to open it. At the same moment, a blinding white ball flashed. He, like the eyes of the devil, peered at me and then swam to you. "

Here we note two things. The ball was moving along the front edge of the wing where the air pressure is maximal. The ball entered the cabin through the hole into which a rocket launcher is inserted. This hole comes out, because of the rocket launcher should launch a rocket outdoor. The pressure in the cabin is higher than outside, because at high altitude where planes fly, the air pressure is small, and the pressure close to normal in is maintained in the cabin. Therefore, the ball, moving in the direction of the gradient of the air density, penetrated into the cabin through the hole into which the rocket launcher was inserted.

Note that in any confined space such as a pipe, BL is moving in the direction opposite to the direction of the airflow. Indeed, in this case, the air flows from high pressure to lower pressure, i.e. in a direction opposite to the pressure gradient. Since the refractive index is proportional to the pressure and BL travels along the gradient of the refractive index, the BL travels along the pressure gradient, and thus in a direction opposite to the direction of air movement. Nearly any gap, through which the air escapes from the interior, there is a region where the refractive index gradient is directed towards this gap. Appearing in this area, BL penetrates through a slot in the cabin, where the refractive index of the air is greater than the outside. The mechanisms, that lead to change shape when BL is passing through the gap,were discussed above. [Torchigin 2003-2005]. Thus, BL is unusual passengers. They can catch a flying plane without a ticket and squeeze into his cabin through a narrow slot.

Simple recommendations can be given to aircraft to BL does not penetrate the aircraft. There should be no gaps in the outer region where the excess air pressure is maximal.

How the ball lightning enters the room through the window panes

Currently, it is well established that BL can penetrate through window glass, sometimes destroying them, but in most cases leaving them intact. A damage, if any, is local in nature and is in that region through which BL penetrated. In work [Bychkov 2004], 42 cases of penetration BL indoors are described. It should be noted that the vast majority of BL theories cannot explain this BL property and therefore must be rejected. This applies to all theories that address any particles: electrons, ions, clusters, plasma and the like. It is known that particles cannot penetrate through glass. Glass flasks and test used in the chemistry, as well as glass cathode ray TV tubes are a good confirmation of this.

There is a list of evidence of eyewitness about Ball Light penetration through windowpanes.

The eyewitness saw a fire ball 10-15 cm in diameter that pass into the room through upper glass, flying slowly in the direction of the nearby table, above which it exploded producing sound as loud as a cannon report. No one suffered, but telephone and electric wires in the room were melted. There was no hole in the window glass through which the ball had passed."

"A few seconds after a close discharge of lightning we saw outside behind a window a bright luminous ball the size of a fist moving downwards along a curved trajectory. This luminous ball passed into the room through the glass of a closed window, moved one meter into the room, made a 90" turn, moved further into the room parallel to the wall and then disappeared with a sharp loud blast. The ball had a violet-and-blue color tinged with red. The observation lasted three seconds. The ball caused no damage either inside or outside the room. After the explosion, there remained an odor typical for electric discharges."

KC-97 USAF tanker airplane was on a blind flight in the clouds at an altitude of 5400 m. There was weak precipitation with a temperature above 0" C. St. Elmo lights appeared at the binding of the front windows. The pilot saw a yellow, white ball penetrates inside through the windscreen passing between him and the second pilot at a speed of a running man. The pilot waited tensely for an explosion to come. The ball flew along the passage, passing the navigator and the flight mechanic. In approximately three seconds, the regulars reported by intercom from the rear compartment that a fireball had rolled through the rear compartment and disappeared into the clouds moving along the right wing. The ball did not produce any sounds.

Suddenly, during a strong discharge, a little ball, that looked very much like a bright electric buBall Light of 100 W, flew in through the window glass. It flew over the elder son's head 0.5 m from him, then lowered a little towards the furnace. The ball moved rather fast, but at the same time somewhat smoothly since we all distinctly saw a bright ball, not just a glaring line. The ball turned back from the furnace and, after flying a little backward, exploded near my feet (15cm above the floor and 8-10 cm from my leg). I was barefoot but felt no heat. As for the sound, it was like someone had smashed an electric bulb. I observed the ball lightning not very long, 3-5 seconds. I stood up to check the glass. It was intact, but from the outside, there remained around dry area, while the rest was all wet with heavy rain."

"During a very severe thunderstorm into the room right through the window glass slowly entered a glaring little ball 4-5 cm in diameter. It passed through the glass without changing its shape as though there was no glass at all. It struck a metal ball decorating the bed, bounced back towards the window and left through the glass as slowly as it had entered. When the ball hit the bed there came a melodious sound similar to the sound of a tuning fork. It all lasted 5-7seconds. The glass, through which the ball passed twice, bore no traces whatsoever."

"I heard a cracking sound coming from the window. I raised my head and saw a fireball 8-10 cm in diameter that flew through the window glass. The ball did not change as it passed through the window. It flew directly at us and blew up between me and my son (approximately 15 cm from me). The sound was like a shot of an air rifle. My son and I were not injured. I found no hole in the window glass."

"Through the double-glass window frame three meters from me a little fire spot entered the room, hung in the air and took the shape of a ball approximately 3 cm in diameter. Its brightness was like that of a 100 W yellow-light electric bulb. It did not move anywhere, just hung there, and later began to turn pale until it faded completely. It all lasted about 6 seconds. Nearby, approximately 70-80 centimeters away, there was a kapron blind and an electric meter, but the ball lightning caused no damage."

"Suddenly, a bright-red fireball approximately 15 cm in diameter entered through the glass in the window. Somewhere in the center of the hall about two meters above the floor it exploded with the sound of a rifle-shot. Sparks fell down cracking throughout the entire hall; the hallwas filled with smoke, it smelled of burned straw. No one got hurt, there was no damage on the glass. It all lasted about 2 seconds."

"Suddenly, a ball lightning 1.5-2 cm in diameter, flew in through a closed window 1.5-2 m from us. The lightning flew in with a loud cracking sound and hung still between us 1 m away. We did not move. Slowly, at the speed of approximately 20 cm/s, it moved towards the door and left through a keyhole. There it discharged exploded loudly. We were afraid to touch the door, but someone opened the door, came in and nothing happened to him. In the next room, a TV set got out of order, though it seemed to us that the lightning exploded right inside the keyhole. We found no damage on the window glass. It all lasted 25-30 sec."

"During a thunderstorm a fire ball flew into a lobby of a hotel through an open window, flew past two executives at a distance of one meter or so and flew out through a closed window leaving a hole in the glass the size of a fist. Some 15steps from the building the fire ball collided with a big silver poplar and exploded chipping off a chip 20 cm wide, 2 cm thick and about 10 meters long. The sound of the explosion was similar to a rifle shot. No one was hurt."

"Suddenly, after a strong discharge, an orange ball the size of a goose egg that shone as a 200 W lamp, flew through the window into the room. Rather slowly, with a cracking sound, it drifted above the table, rolled along a nickel-plated back of the bed, along the strings of a guitar that hung on the wall (the strings immediately started to sound), then again flew right in front of me (half a meter away) above the table and left through the window. It seemed to me that I felt slight heat coming from it. When we recovered from the shock, we examined the window glass and found two perfectly round holes in it the size of the lightning. There were no drops of melted glass. We found nothing wrong with the back of the bed and the strings. There was a light smell of burning in the room. We were watching the ball lightning for approximately 20 seconds."

"Suddenly, the whole sky lit up and a fire-yellow round ball with a blue tinge in the middle flew into the room through the window, crushing the glass. It was 8-10 centimeters in diameter, shone like a 100 W bulb, moved at a 2 m/s speed, crackled and produced smoke. It flew to me, touched the fingers of my right hand. It felt very hot, as if someone stuck a needle into my fingers. Then it flew toward the door that had a 10 x 10 cm hole below for a cat to pass. The ball passed out through the hole into the porch. In the porch there was a separator screwed onto a table, and above it 1.5 m from the floor a shelf nailed to the wall with jars of milk and sour cream on it. At that moment a terrible explosion shook the porch, all jars fell to the floor from the shelf. We were all very frightened, my father rushed to me crying 'Are you alive?'. I said 'I am, but my hand was as if made of cotton. My mother started to rub my hand with liquid ammonia. Daddy went to the porch, and when he returned, he said that there was a smell of rotten apples. Our neighbors came hurrying in and said that they also saw how a 'fire ball' flew into our window. My hand recovered, but it took a long time before I was back to my senses, probably because I was so frightened. There remained a hole in the window glass the size of a plate, its edges blackened a little It all lasted 3-5 seconds."

Once in the summer a powerful thunderstorm broke out, lightning flashed, the rain was heavy and intense. The mother stood on the terrace behind a glass door. Behind her there was another door that led to a machine room. Suddenly, mother saw a white ball tinged with blue, as large as a head of a newborn baby, and it moved directly at her. Mother threw herself aside, the ball drifted slowly past her, leaving neat round holes in the glass in both doors, and moved towards a working machine. There came a peculiar crackle, as if two electric wires came into contact, and the ball disappeared."

"Suddenly, something red flashed in a slot between cooking-rings and a fire-red ball flew out into the room. I understood at once that it was ball lightning. The ball was not big, 7-8 cm in diameter. It started flying back and forth across the room that was 3 m wide. It was approaching me, but not fast. It was flying in the room from wall to wall at low speed. When approaching the wall, the ball did not touch it, but turned back some 15-20 cm from it. The ball itself looked fire red as if it was red hot. Then, the ball headed along the room to the window at the same low speed. Before my eyes, it flew outside through the glass absolutely quietly, without any noise or crackle, and as it was flying outdoors it was the same ball as before. I saw how it left through the glass, but did not notice any diminishing or lengthening while it was passing through the glass. However, a little hole remained in the glass, considerably smaller than the ball's diameter. The hole was of the size of a coin, with cindered edge, melted 0.5 cm outward."

"Aluminous little snake flew through the glass into the room, immediately forming a bright glowing puddle on the floor that vanished right away. A piece of glass was knocked out from the balcony door glass that had the shape of a truncated cone with smaller base approximately 2 mm (inlet hole) and bigger base 6 mm (outlet hole)." "Ball lightning looking like a hairy red ball approximately 5 cm is diameter approached from outside the outer glass of a double-glass window frame of a classroom situated on the second floor of a school building. In the classroom as a teacher and a group of children. A small round hole with luminous red contour was formed in the glass. Then the diameter of the hole enlarged reaching 3-4 cm, and the BL disappeared with a burst of light and loud sound. At the moment when the BL disappeared the teacher who was holding an epidiascope plugged into an electric socket in his hands, experienced electric shock. The BL interacted with glass for approximately 5 seconds. As a result, the internal glass remained intact, while a round hole was formed in the external one."

"Suddenly, lightning flashed and a fireball of the size of a football flew in unexpectedly through the window. It was tinged with red and blue. We could look at it without blinking since it appeared transparent. There was a hole left in the glass 7 by 10 cm with round edges. This fireball was flying under the ceiling slowly and silently as a soap   bubble, producing blue sparking flashes approximately 1 cm long. There were a great number of these flashes flying around. It became stuffy in the room, and blue gas formed. After skirting a samovar covered by a knitted napkin that stood on the table, the ball approached the radio. After this the radio's power supply was burned out. Then, the ball flew outside, breaking the lower glass in the window."

"A golden ball tinged with red of the size of an Antonov apple separated from the window. The ball flew slowly 10 cm above the head of a boy who was sitting at the table, right before the face of a girl, silently hit the side of the cupboard that stood nearby, bounced back, flew close to an electric switch and 'broke' into sparks like a Bengal light. The window glass turned out to be cut as if by a diamond. There was a crack across the side of the cupboard from the bottom to the top. The switch was not damaged. The ball emitted no heat. It all lasted about 30 seconds."

"On the window, somewhere on the glass, appeared something like a soap bubble, as big as a half of a man's palm (no more than 15 cm). As I remember, it was not exactly a ball, but had a slightly pulled-out shape. When inside the house, it 'vibrated' for a second, like a soap bubble before breaking away from a tube. Then it flew from the window along the kitchen past three of us towards the furnace. Maneuvering between us, changing shape, gleaming, it leaped into the furnace and we lost the sight of it in the fire. It might have 'escaped' through the chimney. There was no sound. It was flying not fast (- 1 m/s) and was moving along a curved trajectory carefully skirting us. It lasted 3-4 seconds. My sister and I ran outside to examine the window. In that spot there was a small slot between the glass and the frame, but too narrow even for a mosquito to pass through. There was no trace of a bum or anything like it on the frame. It may have seeped through the slot, but we did not see that. Its color was a pale yellow and pink."

"During a thunderstorm, a yellow and orange ball about 15 cm in diameter   with an undefined permanently vibrating contour crawled into the room through   an open upper part of the window. It was not too bright to look at. Silently and slowly, it rolled along the wall. It rolled over the door where I stood leaning on   the door post to the other room, continued to move towards the window at the opposite side, and crawled outside, squeezing itself through a crack in the glass 1-2 mm wide. The ball flew 20-30 cm above my head. It did not emit any heat. There were no traces left on the wall. It all took place during 1-2 minutes."

"Suddenly, through the double-glass window, a fireball as large as football (25-27 cm in diameter) flew into the room. Inside the ball, I could see a play of different colors: bright red, dark purple, and orange. It resembled the fire of burning wood in a big bonfire or of firewood in a Russian furnace. The ball illuminated the entire room, everything in it. The door to another room was open. Freely and silently, the ball flew across my room and moved rapidly to the next one. After flying 2 meters there, it stopped in the middle of the room. Its appearance changed; now it resembled a white cloud on a blue sky, or smoke, or white colored gas. Then, without moving, it dissolved in the air, disappeared, leaving the smell of burning sulfur. The entire event lasted 2-3 seconds. When I recovered my senses, I stood up, opened the balcony door, and checked all electric devices-everything was all right. The smell in the room lasted for 2 hours."

"During a strong thunderstorm my daughter-in-law and I were sitting at home reading. Suddenly there came a terrible clap of thunder and a fireball, its size6-7 cm, flew in through a closed window. When it was flying in the room there was a loud crackle. After making a circle in the room, the ball flew out through the same window."

"The weather was cloudy, but there was no thunderstorm activity. Around 5p.m. I heard hissing. At the same time, a luminous ball that consisted of double dotted lines 2.5-3 mm thick flew through an open balcony door into the room at the height of 60-80 cm above the floor. Its color may be compared to a heated spiral of an electric stove. The ball (50-60 cm in diameter) started to spin while hanging approximately 50 cm away from the doorstep. The entire ball spun and hissed like a swarm of bees. We did not move. After spinning there for a while, the ball began to move slowly, like a soap bubble in the air, towards the wall. It changed into a conical shape with the sharp end pointing to an electric socket. When it was only a meter from the socket, two continuous 'threads' protruded from the cone's tip into the socket. This produced a loud noise. The entire ball was pulled into the socket. It is difficult to say how long this all lasted, perhaps about a minute. It is surprising, but the electric wiring was not damaged. Suddenly I heard a click behind my back that reminded me of 220 V wires short circuiting. A ball shining with red light, 5-6 cm in diameter, flew between me and my cousin, stopped for awhile near my other cousin who was sitting on my aunt's lap right near the window, and with a light ringing sound slipped into a closed window.There were no traces left, either on the framenor on the glass. An aunt, who sat with her face in the spot where the ball appeared, said that it came out of either a telephone or a radio socket (they were close to each other). The telephone and the radio turned off."

BL detects window just as it detects a hole in the walls because distributions of the air density near the windows and slots are identical. In addition, in fact, in both cases, the gradient of the refractive index of the air should be directed to the room. If the room temperature is lower than outside, the heat penetrates into the room through the window glass. It is known that the heat propagates in a direction opposite the temperature gradient. This means that the temperature gradient directed from the inside to outside. The gradient of the air density is opposite to the gradient of the air temperature and, therefore, is directedinto the room. The nature of the distribution of the air density near a hole, as shown in Fig.6, is preserved for the window. The distribution of air density near a window coincides with the distribution of air density near the window with zero thickness of the glass.

Penetration BL through window glass in the room looks like as follows. If a light beam propagated through a flat glass plate (for example, window pane) the angle of incidence α is equal to angle of transmission β with which the beam exits the plate from the opposite side (see Fig. 8) on condition that refractive indexes of optical mediums before and after propagation through the plate are identical. It would seem that the light beam propagates in a straight line in the room after penetration through the windowpane and cannot get back into the BL shell. This is true if the refractive indexes of the air on both sides of the plate are the same.

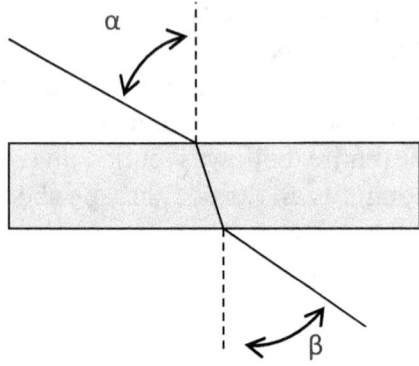

Fig. 8. Propagation of a light beam through a plane transparent plate

However, the refractive index of the compressed air in the shell BL is greater than the refractive index of air on the opposite side of the plate where the normal air pressure takes place. In this case, $\alpha < \beta$. When BL touches on the surface of the glass plate, we have $\alpha=90^0$. In this case, angle β should be greater than 90^0. It is impossible. There is the total internal reflection from the surface of the glass in the room as is shown in Fig. 9. Thus, there are two modes. In the first mode, the total internal reflection from the outer surface takes place. In the second mode, the light passes through glass.

When BL touches the surface of the glass, there is a second mode because $\alpha=90^0$. As is seen in Fig. 9, the light beam returns back into the first medium. However, the region where the incident beam enters the plate and the region where the reflected beam

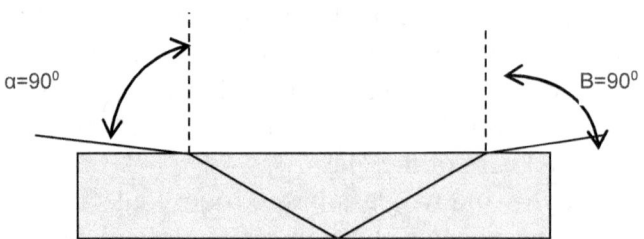

Fig. 9. Total inner reflection from bottom surface of a glass plate

leaves the plate are different. A distance between these regions is comparable with the width of the plate. Seemingly, the reflected beam cannot return to BL shell. Possibly, the similar situation takes place in nature, and BL in this case does not penetrate through a glass plate. But many attempts are given to BL. The situation presented in Fig. 10a is possible. In this case, BL nearing the windowpane heats it due to light radiation and inevitable dissipative losses in the glass because its transparency is not absolute. As a result, BL takes a form shown in Fig. 10a. In this case, the light can returninto the BL shell after the total internal reflection from the outer side of the glass.

A strong electromagnetic field occurs in the layer of the air near the surface of the glass in the room. Letter P in Fig 10a shows a position of this layer. The thickness of this layer is comparable with the average wavelength of white light and is approximately equal to 1 μm. This field cannot excite the light wave propagating in a room due to the phenomenon of total internal reflection. At the same time, this field can compress the air in this layer due to the electrostriction effect. The refractive index of the compressed air is greater than that of uncompressed one. The next portion of the light that is circulating in the BL shell penetrates into the area of the compressed air. This leads to an increase in its volume, as shown in Figure 10b. In this case, the light begins to propagate in

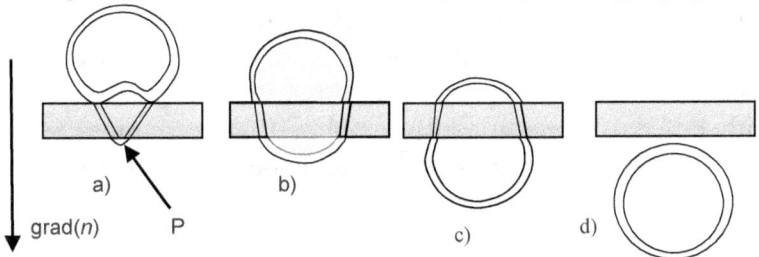

Fig.10. Stages of penetration of the Ball Light shell through the window pane
 a) initial stage of penetration when the region of the compressed air is produced on the back side of the window pane
 b) intermediate stage when a smaller part of the Ball Light shell penetrated on the back side in the room
 c) intermediate stage when a greater part of the Ball Light shell penetrated on the back side in the room
 d) Ball Light penetrated in the room completely

the glass according to the first mode.

If air densities are different on opposite sides of the glass pane, BL is moving in the direction where the density of the air is greater in accordance with the above-described effect. It seems that the BL easily passes through the glass. In fact, only light passes through the glass. After that, it forms a layer of compressed air on the opposite side of the glass from the air in the room. A sequence of steps of BL penetration through a glass pane is shown in Figs. 10.

As is seen, the light within Ball Light shell is circulating through both outer and internal sides of the windowpane. But the compressed air in the BL shell located in the outer side of the window pane does not penetrate in the BL shell located in the internal side of the glass. Light cannot be odorous. Therefore, any odors cannot penetrate through glass. An odor after BL disappearance may refer to the smell that arose when BL heated any objects inside the room.

Some evidence indicate that the BL before enter the room, repeatedly bounce off the glass. Thisis explained by the fact that the glass is heated due to radiation. In this case, BL bounces off the glass as from conventional opaque obstacle. There is evidence that if the glass is chipped off or there is a gap in the window, and then the BL comes through this gap. In this case BL changes its shape in the same manner as BL penetrates through the usual hole. The number of reported cases, when BL penetrates through the crack in the window, is compared with a number of cases where BL penetrates directly through the glass. As the number of windows with defects is significantly smaller than a number of windows with conventional panes, it can be concluded that the presence of defects increases a probability of BL penetration through a window.

As for the heating of glass during the passage of BL, the result depends on many parameters such as the intensity of BL light, the losses in the pane, the presence of dirt on the pane, thickness of the pane, etc.Having analyzed the features of the resulting holes in the pane, we can conclude that the paneis heated rapidly enough, and the heating is localized in a circle, through which BL penetrates. Assuming that the rate of passage through the pane is constant, we can see that the maximum heating occurs at the circle whose diameter equals the BL diameter.

Behavior of the ball lightning near metal objects

There are numerous reports that BL is attracted to a metal object, such as a fence of metal bars or telephone wires. Approaching a metal object, BL usually starts moving along the object. Let us try to explain the behavior of this feature BL, bearing in mind that the BL is moving along a gradient of refractive index.

It is known that metals are not only good conductors of electric current, but also good conductors of heat that is characterized by high thermal conductivity. The temperature of different objects on the surface of the earth varies due to diurnal variations of air temperature. On a sunny day, the temperature of the upper layers of the earth's surface is higher than deeper layers. For example, if a metal column is embedded in the ground, the temperature of the column is less than the ambient air, as the heat that the column receives from the surrounding air, propagates down into dug into the ground portion of the column. As a result, the gradient of the refractive index of the air near the column is directed towards the bottom of the column. BL appearing near the column starts moving towards the bottom of the column. If the gradient of the refractive index is not perpendicular to the column axis, the BL will move along the column at a certain distance from its surface with local heating the column.

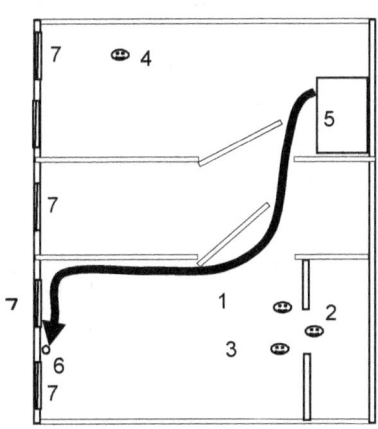

Fig.11 Trace of BL from the oven to the grounded metallic rod

Generally, the law of uniform in mechanics holds for BL also. Indeed, if the BL is moving in a certain direction in an uniform air, then it leaves the warmer air behind it. The gradient of the refractive index arises that ensures further BL motion.

For example, the Stakhanov [Stakhanov 1996] in the case of 8 describes the observation, in which the two BL jumped out of the oven 5 (Fig. 11), passed through two doors, passed along two walls and pulled to ground 6 in a form of a metal wire. Their trajectory is shown in Figure 11. The motion of BL is observed by four observers: 1, 2, 3, 4. Approaching the metal wire 6 near windows 7, BL changed its shape, becoming a prelate ellipsoid, penetrated through the gap between the wire and the floor and disappeared. That is exactly what should be happening if keep in mind the above-mentioned features of the motion BL indoors and near metal objects.

In some cases, the interaction of BL with a metal object acquires a different character. This occurs when the geometry of a metal object such that BL can heat metal. For example, BL is in contact with the end of the metal wire. In this case, the conditions of heat propagation in the metal differ from the case when the BL may be in contact with metallic body having comparable sizes in all three dimensions. In the first case, the heat can be distributed in one dimension - along the wire. In the second case, the heat can be distributed in three dimensions. Therefore, in the first case, heating of the metal at the point of contact is much greater than in the second.

If the metal temperature is increased so that its evaporation begins, then the reflective index in the region where the BL contacts with the metal is increased due to adding to the region the metal vapor. As a result, BL «sticks" to the area. BL will vaporize the wire until it is over, or until

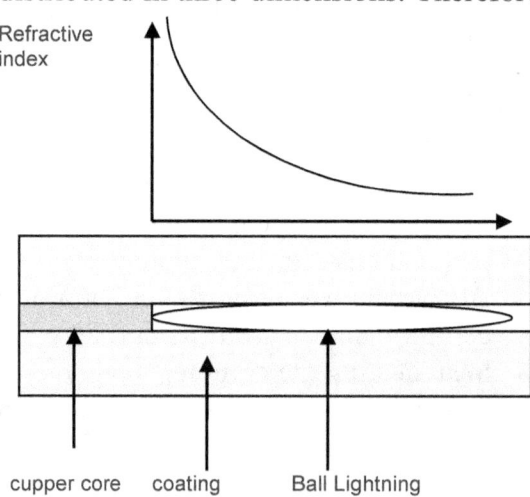

cupper core   coating   Ball Lightning

Fig. 12 Burning cupper core of TV cable by Ball Lightning

BL energy is exhausted. This picture has numerous confirmations.

The following case in this respect is very revealing. Thunder ball burnt out the TV cable with copper core and polyethylene shell at a distance of several meters, leaving the shell almost intact. This fact is easily explained. The metal inside the shell is evaporated so quickly that the area with high temperature is moved along the cable at high speed. This heats only a small area of the inner shell, directly

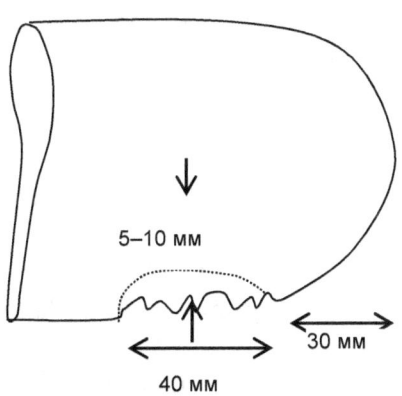

Fig. 13. Damage of a blade of the propeller by Ball Lightning

adjacent to the metal core. The heat did not have time to spread to the entire mass of the shell. The highest pressure and thus highest refractive index are near the end of the wire evaporated. Therefore, BL has a form of a thin sausage located near the end of the wire during the whole process of evaporation as is shown in Fig. 12.

The witness saw after extremely strong lightning strikes a telephone pillar on the street rolled bright mass of 1 m in diameter, and behind it a few more smaller balls [Singer 1971]. Later it was discovered that a wire between two pillars interrupted and a significant chunk lacks.

In another case, a very strong lightning strike destroyed the copper antenna shortly after it was installed for the study of thunderstorm electricity.

The witness, who watched the storm, saw a big ball of fire, apparently formed due to vaporize 65 m two-millimeter wire.

Stakhanov in case No. 4 describes the case where BL burnt out hole diameter of 5 mm and a depth of 3 mm at the end of the cleaning rod, attached to the gun. It is noted that no trace of fusion was observed. Metal just disappeared. Therefore, it should be since the metal must evaporate to BL remained about metal.

In the description of aircraft collisions with BL is often reported that during the examination of the aircraft several damaged or melted rivets in front of the fuselage are revealed [Singer 1971].Thisis easily explained if we bear in mind that the rivet located on the smooth surface of the fuselage breaks uniform airflow over the fuselage. An excess pressure raised near the rivet, and there is a local maximum of the density of air. Finding itself in this maximum, BL vaporizes a portion of the rivet. Thus, the same mechanisms leading to the evaporation of long metal cylinder take place. Evaporation takes place until the protruding portion of the rivet disappears. This leads to the disappearance of the excess pressure produced by the protruding portion of the rivet.

Very curious pattern is in the book by Singer [Singer 1971], which shows the results of the interaction of BL with the propeller blades (Fig. 13). Because the propeller pulls the plane forward, the propeller is undergone by the overpressure. This is the maximum pressure in that part of the blade, where the violation of the blade edge occurred. Located in an area with a maximum pressure, BL rotates with the blade and burns the craters on it, just as it burns craters on fixed metal objects.

Why the ball lightning whistles and causes radio interference

In the steady state, BL form is unchangeable, and it does not excite any acoustic waves. If BL is considered as an elastic membrane, its shell has a plurality of eigen frequencies for various types of mechanical oscillations. These oscillations can be excited by various irregularities, in particular, the dust particles, which are foundon the BL way. Depending on how these eigen frequencies are distributed over a low frequency range and which of them are excited in reality, BL may emit different sounds.

As for radio interferences, many witnesses say that, indeed, BL creates interference [Dmitriev 1967], [Stakhanov 1996]. But this does not mean that the BL emits radio waves. Cod from BL can be heard in the handset [Stakhanov 1996], which, as we know, cannot receive radio waves. We can offer the following explanation. As will be shown below, BL may carry an electrical charge. Changing its shape at audio frequencies, BL causes changes in the distribution of the electric field in the surrounding space. Such redistribution is also responsible for the electrical effects arising at the BL explosion. These effects cause a crack in the radio and the handset. A similar crackling can be heard in the radio when turning on or off the Ball Light.

Why the ball lightning of large diameter takes the form of a flying saucer

Consider what shape acquires BL of several meters in diameter. In the stationary state BL is located in the air layer, where the air density is maximal. The upper and lower poles are located in layers in which the gradient of the density of the air is directed to the layer with maximal density, that is to the equator (Figure 14). As a result, there are forces that tend to squeeze BL. The forces that provide spherical BL are relatively small and decrease as the diameter increases. At the same time, the forces that tend to squeeze BL, increase with increasing diameter. Indeed, the gradient of the refractive index is zero at the equator. The gradient should increase with increasing distance from the equator. Thus, the larger the BL diameter, the greater its tendency to be squeezed. As a result, BL takes the shape of an oblate spheroid. If the distributions of the gradient of the refractive index above and below the equator are different, the flattenings of the top and bottom of the BL are also different. As a result, BL takes the form of the body of revolution, which resembles a saucer or plate.

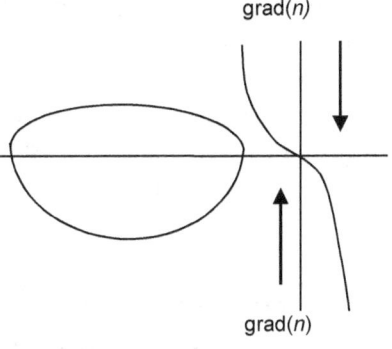

grad(*n*)

grad(*n*)

Fig. 14. Form of the light ball of great diameter located in the air layer where the air refractive index has a maximum. Dependence of the gradient of the refractive index on the height is shown at the right hand

It is known that UFOs can move with great speed and change direction of their speed so sharply that the overload arising in this case is not permitted for living beings. If UFO is BL, it can move with great speed, provided that the gradient of the refractive index in the atmosphere is sufficiently large (in particular, it can catch up a flying aircraft). In that case, if the atmosphere is non-stationary, BL can meet the region in which the direction of the gradient of air density varies quite dramatically. In such areas BL dramatically change the direction of its motion.

Why ball lightnings may have different colors

It is known that the color BL may be very different. The simplest explanation of this fact is the following. The temperature of the region where BL is formed can be very different depending on the conditions under which gas discharge occurs. As is known, the maximal range of the wavelength spectrum is shifted to shorter wavelengths with increasing temperature. Since BL is a combination of compressed gas and the intense electromagnetic radiation, and the maximum of the spectrum of electromagnetic radiation may vary within wide limits, the BL color, which is determined by the maximum of this range, may also be between wide limits.

This simple explanation may impose various subtleties. For instance, the BL color can be shifted towards short wavelengths if BLs are formed by multiple mergers of miniature BL of small diameter, radiation losses of which depends on the wavelength of light circulating in them. Such BLs lose the radiation in the long-wavelength part of the spectrum. As a result, their spectrum shifts to the shorter part. Most BL, formed from the merger of numerous miniature BL, has a purple tint. Such BL observed in experiments [Klimov 1993, 1994].

The disappearance of ball lightning

BL disappears when it becomes unstable (although the stability of the BL is highly conditional, because of the constant reduction of the stored energy in the BL exclude any steady state). Since processes involving light have relatively small time constants, the development process of instability occurs relatively quickly. At some time, a decrease in the intensity of the circulating light leads to a decreaseof air pressure in the BL shell and hence to a decrease in the refractive index. This in turn leads to a further increase of radiation loss and a more rapid reduction in the intensity of the circulating light. At some time instant, the circulating light abruptly leaves BL shell and is radiated in all directions of free space. The source of electrostriction pressure disappears. As a result, the air begins to expand. The time constant of this process is determined by the speed of sound in air, which is 6 orders of magnitude smaller than the speed of light. Pretty often is reported that a sound like a pistol shot heard with the disappearance of BL. This indicates that there is a small amount of compressed air and that the air compression is sufficiently strong. If BL disappears silently, it means that the BL shell is formed by gases the refractive index of which is greater than that of conventional air (see below).

How the ball lightning is catching up a flying aircraft

Potentially dangerous encounters with fireballs occur not only near and above storms, but also on clear weather days. The following mix of cases, both new and historical, are taken from the top-secret report of Oak Ridge National Laboratories. Many such cases exist, but most go unreported [Sagan 1994].

An electrical engineer, Tim served in the Air Force and now was a manager at a micro-networking firm in Worcester, Massachusetts. He described how he saw a two-foot orange fireball aboard a huge jet tanker carrying jet fuel, used for mid-air refueling of other aircraft by means of a boom and fuel line. This fireball floated out to the rear of the aircraft and off into the air. This thoroughly terrified the crew because they were carrying a full load of volatile jet fuel.

Other Air Force crewmen also described fireballs. Robert C, a former director of engineering instruction at Centronics—the once-world-famous computer printer-manufacturer in Nashua, New Hampshire—previously served in the Air Force. In 1977, he described to your author the fireballs seen by air force crews flying jets and tankers. He himself saw a fireball roll on a New York hill.

Inter-storm fireball briefly visits military flight. While flying between lightning storms, I saw a blue-white fireball float through the aircraft. It disappeared after four seconds. Another crewmember also saw it.

USAF and Saint Andrew's Light. I saw what we in the Air Force referred to as "Saint Andrew's Light," or a glowing fireball moving at a constant speed at high altitude. There was no concurrent lightning.

Ball chases flight attendant. While working the day shift—there was considerable thunderstorm activity—meteorologist-in-charge of the National Weather Service Office in Rochester, NY, Peter R. Chastor, was meeting an acquaintance who was a commercial airline pilot, who just had a disturbing encounter. While the airliner was on decent to the airport during the storm, a basketball-sized "ball of sparks" entered through the engine intake. After moving into the fuselage, it chased a screaming flight attendant down the aisle. It vanished before it struck her. This upset the passengers.

Orange ball explodes, rocks airliner. A commercial TWA airliner at two-mile altitude flying from Paris to Cairo passed through a cloudy region. Startled passengers watched as a softball-sized ball of orange-yellow fire rose from under the cabin. The bright rotating ball, surrounded by a thin bluish mist, left a small trail as it moved next to the fuselage. It was only a few feet from the window as it flew alongside the plane. The passengers watched the fireball when it burst into against red "spray" that momentarily shot forward for ten feet and then silently vanished. A loud explosion rocked the plane.

Fireball burns captain, explodes. The former Deputy Director of the British Meteorological Office was flying during summer to Iraq through dense nimbostratus clouds over the Toulouse Gap at 8,500 feet. A fireball popped through cockpit window, burned the terrified captain, and glided through the forward cabin. The ball then entered the rear cabin, and while floating down the aisle, it exploded.

Fireball damages transport. A twin-engine Russian transport plane on August 12 at 12:30 flew near Nizh, Tambosk, 55 miles northeast of Komsomol'sk and 400 miles southeast of Moscow. Dense cumulus and cumulonimbus clouds filled the sky. Pilots Dubinski and Sergienko had seen several showers and storms. At 12:45 they flew into a heavy dark cloud. A dark red, almost orange, ten-inch fireball shot straight for the port side of the cockpit. The fireball came within one meter of the nose, swerved to the port, and circled the running light. It hit the engine, exploded in a blinding white flash, and a flaming band passed along the left side of the fuselage. The explosion sounded like "the explosion of a torpedo in water, muffled and sharp." After landing, the ground crew discovered several melted rivets and two one-inch holes punched into the elevator's trailing edge.

Fireball vaporizes fuselage holes. In 1984, the Russian news agency reported that a four-inch fireball entered a Russian passenger airliner, flew above the passengers' heads and departed out the tail section, leaving two holes in the craft. It appeared on the fuselage, at the front of the cockpit. The ball disappeared with prodigious roar, only to re-emerge seconds later, piercing through an airtight metal wall, entering the passengers' lounge. After it flew about the passengers 'heads, it entered the tail section and split into "two glowing crescents." These two then joined and silently departed the plane. US National Weather meteorologist Peter R. Chaston noted that mechanics later discovered two fuselage holes at entry and exit.

Not only can fireballs squeeze through existing tiny apertures, such as skeleton keyholes, they can vaporize their own holes of entry and departure in metal. Ball lightning has floated down the aisle of commercial airliners and penetrated sheet metal and exited through the metal skin and then bounced outside along the wing, despite the tremendous air resistance, and then flew off.

Your author examined under a microscope and photographed a hole melted through a metal sheet by a fireball, and from the heat of vaporization, then calculated the energy (described elsewhere in the Lawrence Leach case) needed for such metal vaporization.

Blue fireball floats down aisle. It was five minutes past midnight early on March 18, when the flight out of New York to Washington was struck by lightning. The entire airliner was engulfed in a brilliant flash, and the crash awoke sleeping passengers. Seated up front, a scientist from the University of Kent Electronics Laboratory in Canterbury of Kent in England described what the passengers saw.

After a glowing eight-inch sphere appeared at the pilot's cabin, the bluish-white fireball floated down the aisle, past—passing 16 inches from the scientist—and continued on a level path of two-and-a-half feet above the floor at constant speed of three-to-five feet per second, to the plane's rear and silently vanished. Although the fireball came close to several passengers, none felt any heat. With an almost-solid appearance, the ball was optically thick and in perfect equilibrium.

Orange fireball hits jet's nose, destroys electronics. A jet trainer preparing to land at Moody Air Force Base in Georgia encountered lightning. To avoid the storm, they were told to proceed to Mobile, Alabama. When they rolled out onto a westerly heading at 13,120 feet, a big orange ball of fire hit the nose head-on. An explosion shook the craft with such violence the pilots were sure it was a mid-air collision. The ground crew discovered the electronics had melted.

Fireball injures passengers. In a well-publicized encounter, an airliner flying from New York to San Juan, Puerto Rico, was flying off the Florida coast near Jacksonville when the pilots saw a "big fireball advancing with tremendous speed." To avoid a collision, the captain shot his airliner upwards at a steep angle,

Orange ball explodes, rocks airliner. A commercial TWA airliner at two-mile altitude flying from Paris to Cairo passed through a cloudy region. Startled passengers watched as a softball-sized ball of orange-yellow fire rose from under the cabin. The bright rotating ball, surrounded by a thin bluish mist, left a small trail as it moved next to the fuselage. It was only a few feet from the window as it flew alongside the plane. The passengers watched the fireball when it burst into against red "spray" that momentarily shot forward for ten feet and then silently vanished. A loud explosion rocked the plane.

Fireball burns captain, explodes. The former Deputy Director of the British Meteorological Office was flying during summer to Iraq through dense nimbostratus clouds over the Toulouse Gap at 8,500 feet. A fireball popped through a cockpit window, burned the terrified captain, and glided through the forward cabin. The ball then entered the rear cabin, and while floating down the aisle, it exploded.

The following case that has occurred in the Vologda area in February 1946 is rather indicative. The second pilot has seen how on the right wing of the plane about green fire there was a bright white sphere. It has thought that there was a short circuit of an electric lamp, but flash has not disappeared, as usually happens. The sphere has slowly spread on the frontal edge of the wing and has disappeared under the nose part of the machine. Then loud crash was heard and black smoke entered the pilot cabin. Communication was broken. The commander asks the navigator: " Nikolay, can you have noticed where from the sphere was rolled out? " In fact it has appeared directly near your legs" The navigator has answered: "I have taken the gun for rocket to check up, what color a charge within it. But I had no time to open it. The blinding white sphere has flashed at the very same time. It, as an eye of a devil, peered at me, and then has floated to you".

We should note here two circumstances. The sphere moved along a frontal edge of a wing, where pressure of air as much as possible. The sphere has got into a cabin through the hole into which a gun for rocket is inserted. This hole is designated to push rockets outdoor and, therefore, the hole is a tunnel between indoor and outdoor spaces. The air pressure in a cabin of the plane is greater than that outdoor, because air is rarefied at the great height where planes fly. In the same time, the air pressure in the cabin of the plane is supported to the pressure close to normal one for comfort of pilots. Therefore, the sphere, moving in the direction of the gradient of the air density, has got into a cabin through a hole into which the gun for rocket is inserted.

It is informed often enough about collisions of planes with BL. The damaged or melted off rivets in a forward part of a fuselage are noticed at inspection of the plane [Singer 1971]. It is easy to explain it if to mean, that the rivet edged on a smooth surface of a fuselage breaks a uniform flow air near fuselage. Excess pressure is created near the rivet, and there is a local maximum of the air density. Having got in this maximum, Ball Light evaporates a part of the rivet. Thus, action is explained by the same mechanisms that are responsible for evaporation of long metal cylinders. Evaporation takes place until the edged part of a rivet disappears that leads to a disappearance of the excess pressure created by edged part of a rivet.

Very curious figure in the book Singer [Singer 1971], which shows the results of the interaction of BL with propeller blades (Fig. 13). Since the propeller pulls the plane forward, the propeller is subject to the exess pressure. There is the maximum pressure in that part of the blade, where the blade edge breach occurred. Having located in an area with a maximum pressure, BL rotates with the blade and the burns craters on it, just as BL burns the craters on the fixed metal objects.In our opinion, explanation of mechanisms which enable BL to catch up and accompany airplanes is a strong argument in favor of optical nature of Ball Lightning. Objects consisting of any particles cannot accompany an airplane. They must be blown out by a stream of running air immediately. On the contrary, it does not matter for light circulating in the space where air pressure is maximal regardless of motionless or moving air produces the excess pressure, because the speed of moving air is smaller by million times than the light speed.

Since BL falls on the ground, then we can assume that the probability to meet BL near the surface of the earth is greater than that at the height at which airplanes fly. Why does BL prefer to visit flying aircraft (there are numerous reports) and completely indifferent to buses, to trains, to airplanes on the ground? Anyone who watched from the window of an airplane and pay attention to the small clouds that are carried with great speed back may ask why is BL hasn't blown from the airplane wing by the hurricane, the speed of which is several times higher than the strongest hurricane on earth? If the Ball Light is comprised of any particles, clusters, ions, electrons, and so on, all this should be immediately pulled away.

The answer is quite simple. The flying aircraft provides an inhomogeneity of the refractive index in the air atmosphere. The excessive air pressure near the leading edge of the aircraft wing is 0.2 atmospheres at aircraft speed of 720 km/h [Torchigin 2004 Phys. Lett.]. This creates a positive pressure in the vicinity of the aircraft. The gradient of the refractive index near the aircraft is greatin such degree that it provides BL motion at a speed that

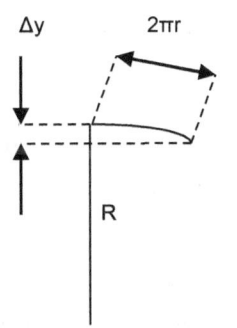

Fig.15 Deflection Δy of a light beam propagating in an inhomogeneous optical medium

exceeds the speed of the aircraft. As a result, BL located in the vicinity of the aircraft can catch up it.

Let us estimate preliminary the velocity at which a ball light moves in an inhomogeneous atmosphere. Note at once that the velocity may be enormous. For example, if we assume that Ball Light of 10 cm diameter is shifted by 1μm per one light revolution, then the ball light is shifted by 1km because the light within the ball light performs 10^9 revolutions per second. Indeed, the length of one circulation is 0.3 m, and the light speed is $3 \cdot 10^8$ m/c.

If the gradient of the air refractive index grad(n) is perpendicular to the direction of propagating of a light beam, the beam is curved in the direction of the gradient. The radius of the curvature is equal $R=1/\text{grad}(n)$. For example, if $R=100$ km in the desert then grad(n)=10^{-5} m^{-1}.

Let the cylindrical layer of r radius and the axis paralleled to the z-axis be located in an inhomogeneous atmosphere. Let the refractive index of the atmosphere increase along the y-axis at the rate grad(n)= dn/dy> 0 and do not depend on x, z coordinates (Fig. 15). In this case, the rotating light deflects in the direction of the y axis and, therefore, the cylindrical layer moves gradually along the y-axis. Its shift per one rotation can be equal roughly to the shift of a recliner light beam that propagates at the distance equaled to the perimeter of the ball light $2\pi r$. As is seen in Fig.15, deflection Δy is given by $R[1-\text{Cos}(\varphi)]$ where $\varphi<<1$ and $\varphi=2\pi r/R$. Since $\text{Cos}(\varphi)=\approx1-\varphi^2/2$ in this case, we have

$$\Delta y = 2\pi^2 r^2 / R \qquad (2)$$

Shift Δy takes place in time interval $T=2\pi rn/c$. Then the velocity of the ball light is given by

$$v = c\pi r / R = c\pi r / R = c\pi r \, grad(n) = c\pi \Delta n_D / 2 \tag{3}$$

where $\Delta n_D = grad(n)D$ is a change of the air refractive index at the distance equaled to the diameter of the ball light. As is seen, the velocity is proportional to the diameter of the ball light. We have not taken into account the fact that the displacement of the light beam is smaller if $grad(n)$ is not perpendicular to the direction of propagation of light. This fact has been taken into account in [Torchigin 2004 Phys. Lett.]. In this case the velocity is smaller and is given by

$$v = \frac{grad(n)rc}{2} = \frac{\Delta n_D c}{4} \tag{4}$$

For example, for $\Delta n_D = 10^{-5}$, we have $v = 750 \text{m/s}$, that is v surpasses the sound speed in air.

Ought to underline that ball light movement is not accompanied by movement of the air compressed within it. Like ball light movement through a windowglass, where only light radiation penetrates through the glass and compresses new air portion located at the opposite side, lightbubble movement in the air atmosphere is accompanied by compression of new air portions on the front side and the corresponding release of air portions on the rear side.

Now let us estimate a degree of atmosphere in homogeneity produced by a flying airplane. Anadditionalairpressure Δp near a front edge of a wing where the air speed relative to the airplane is equal to zero and is equal to the airplane speed u relatively the earth is determined by the following expression

$$\Delta p = \frac{\rho u^2}{2} \tag{5}$$

where ρ is the air density and $\rho \sim= 1 \text{ kg/m}^3$. At the airplane speed $u = 720 \text{ km/h} = 200 \text{ m/s}$ we have $\Delta p = 2 \times 10^4 \text{Pa} \sim= 0.2$ atmospheres. The air refractive index at the normal atmospheric pressure is determined by the expression $n = 1 + \Delta n$, where $\Delta n =$

2.7×10^{-4}. Since the air density is proportional to the air pressure, then

$$n(\Delta p) = 1 + \frac{\Delta p}{p_0} \Delta n$$

(6)

where p_0 is the air pressure at normal conditions. From (6) we have that an increase in the air pressure by $\Delta p = 0.2$ atmospheres entails increasing in the air refractive index by $\Delta n\,(\Delta p) = 0.2\Delta n \sim = 0.54 \times 10^{-4}$.

As follows from (4), to provide ball light motion at the air plane speed it is necessary the following air inhomogeneity $\Delta n_D = u/(c/4) \cong 2.66 \times 10^{-6}$. Under the assumption that Δp decreases linearly with distance from the air plane, we obtain that the such decrease takes place at the distance

$$S \cong \frac{\Delta n(\Delta p)}{\Delta n_D} D = 20D$$

(7)

At $D = 0.1$ m, we obtain that bubbles may catch up the airplane located from them at a distance $S = 2$ m. Needless to say, it is very rough estimations determining the order of magnitude only. However, they show that a flying airplane attracts all ball lights located directly ahead, as well as to the right, left, at the top and bottom in the region of inhomogeneous atmosphere produced by airplane. Achieving the airplane, ball light stops in the region where the air density is maximal and moves with this region together and, therefore, with the airplane. No airplane maneuvers can separate the ball light and airplane. Ought to note that the additional air pressure Δp near front edge of the wing is proportional to the square of airplane speed u, that is the region from which ball lights are attracted to the airplane increases with an increase in the airplane speed. Besides, the probability for the airplane to meet any BLs is proportional to the airplane speed. Indeed, if the airplane could make several revolutions around the Earth per one second, it could gather all BLs that were met at its trace. Are there any other hypothesizes that explain how BLs can pursue an airplane and moves together with it?

As is known, the air is rarefied at great height where airplanes fly. Because of this additional pressure is generated in airplane cabins and saloons to provide a normal breath for passengers. Since it is very hard and is not justified economically to keep these rooms hermetic absolutely, there is an air compressor that continuously pumps in the outdoor air. It is natural enough to take the air from that region where the air pressure is maximal that is from the region where BLs can be located. A turbine compressor pumps the air, and there is a tunnel between the salon and outdoor at any position of turbine blades. Since the ball light layer width is several micrometers only, a split of width smaller than ten micrometers is sufficient for a ball light penetration. The air density gradient is directed into the salon. Moving along the gradient, BL penetrates in the salon. Mechanisms that enable BL to change its shape are considered in [Torchigin 2003-2004]. One can give a recommendation to airplane designers to avoid BL penetration. There must be no splits in the region where additional air pressure is maximal.

Ball Light is located in the region where the gradient of the refractive index is such that it provides the Ball Light motion at a speed equal to the speed of the aircraft. It is easily seen that the position of the Ball Light in this region is stable. The region is located near the leading edge of the aircraft wing. Ball Light moves with the region and therefore moves together with the aircraft. No aircraft maneuvers can separate Ball Light from the aircraft. Maximum Ball Light speed is determined by the maximum of the gradient of the refractive index produced by the aircraft and is greater than the maximum speed of the aircraft. Therefore, Ball Light remains in the region near the maximum refractive index, regardless of the air speed in the region. Therefore, Ball Light cannot be blown out from the region.

In our opinion, the explanation of the mechanisms that allow the Ball Light to catch up and accompany an aircraft is a strong argument in favor of the optical nature of the BL. No objects consisting of particles can accompany the aircraft. They will immediately blow out by airflow. It does not matter for the light circulating in the region with the highest refractive index whether there is fixed and moving air because the speed of the moving air is negligible small as compared with the speed of light (one million times smaller than the speed of light).

The probability of an aircraft to meet any Ball Light in its track is proportional to its speed. Indeed, if the plane could fly around the earth in one second, he would gather all the Ball Light encountered it during this time. That is why BLs are observed in flying aircrafts rather than in aircrafts standing in airports. Are there other hypotheses about the BL nature, which could explain how the Ball Light can catch a plane and go along with it? We are not aware of such hypotheses.

Conclusion

We have shown that properties of Ball Light derived from well-known laws of physics and optics are identical with properties of natural Ball Lightnings obtained from numerous evidence of eyewitnesses. We hope that the reader, having read this book, will recognize that our notion about the natural Ball lightning works and the BL nature has been discovered. Certainly, it is hard to believe that a self-confined light in a form of Ball Light can exist in the nature. Nobody even hinted about such a possibility.

Should recognize that the properties of the Ball Light and its behavior in the atmosphere can be quite unexpected. Mysterious and inexplicable behavior of natural Ball Lightnings tell us about the possible features of the Ball Light behavior. Having analyzed these features on the basis of known laws of physics presented in the beginning of the book, we were pleased to note that the behavior of the Ball Light completely coincides with the mysterious and intriguing behavior of natural Ball Lightnings.

Unfortunately, a generally accepted notion about optically induced forces that play a decisive role in the BL existence and its intriguing behavior are absent at present. Because of this, it is impossible to hope that our theory will win a general recognition in the nearest future.

Above century was required for the Copernicus theory to win a general recognition. A general sense spokes that the Sun and stars move but the Earth is motionless. Only scientific knowledge enabled to override this misconception.

References

2002 Torchigin V.P. 2002. About stability of spherical layers of compressed air formed by intense light. Investigated in Russia. Electronic Journal. http://zhurnal.ape.relarn.ru/articles/2002/093.pdf (In Russian).

2003 Torchigin V. P. On the nature of Ball Lightning, Doclady Physics vol. 48, no. 3 pp. 108-11 (2003).

2003 Torchigin V. P., 2003 Optical Resonators in the Atmosphere. Laser Physics 13, no. 6, 919–931. 2003

2003 Torchigin V.P., A.V. Torchigin An increase in the wavelength of the light pulses propagating through a fiber. Physics Letters A, 311 (2003) 21.

2003 Torchigin, V. P. Lomonosov; 2003 no.2, 86-90.

2003 Torchigin, V. P., Torchigin, A. V. Chemistry and life, 2003, № 1, 12–15.

2003 Torchigin, V. P., Torchigin, A. V. Propagation of self-confined Light radiation in Inhomogeneous Air. PhysicaScripta, 2003, 68, 388–393.

2003. Torchigin V. P., Torchigin S. V., 2003 Optical solitons at propagation of whispering gallery waves. Quantum Electronics, 33 (10), (2003), 913–918.

2003. Torchigin V. P., V.A. Suchugov, I.K. Krasuyk et al., 2003 Change in the wavelength of light radiation stored within an optical resonator by means of an acoustic pulse. Optics

2004 Torchigin V. P. Acousto-optical devices USA patent number 6771412 of 3 August 2004.

2004 Torchigin V.P., Torchigin A.V. Behavior of self-confined layer of light radiation in the air atmosphere. Phys. Lett. A. 2004, 328/2–3, 189–195.

2004 Torchigin, V. P. Manifestation of Optical Quadratic Nonlinerity in Gas Mixtures. Physics; 2004, 49, No.10, 553–555

2004 Torchigin, V. P., Torchigin A. V., Space soliton in gas mixtures. Opt. Comm. 2004 240/4-6, 449-455

2004 Torchigin, V. P., Torchigin, A. V. Mechanism of the Appearance of Ball Lightning from Usual Lightning. Doclady Physics; 2004, 49, No. 9, 494–495

2004. Torchigin V. P., Torchigin A. V., 2004 Role of Ball Lightnings in Low Energy Nuclear Reactions. Infinite Energy 54, (2004), 46–50

2005 Torchigin V. P., A. V. Torchigin, 2005 Physical Nature of Ball lightning. European physical Journal D 36, (2005), 319–327.

2005 Torchigin V.P., A.V. Torchigin, Features of Ball Lightning stability, Europhysics Journal D 2005, 32, 383–389.

2005 Torchigin V.P., A.V. Torchigin, Phenomenon of ball Lightning and its outgrowth. Phys. Lett. A; 2005, 337, 112–120.

2006 Torchigin V.P. Is it possible to consider the Ball lightning as a reason of the Chernobyl tragedy? Bulletin of Atomic Energy 84 89-92.

2007 Torchigin, V. P., Torchigin, A. V. Self-organization of intense light within erosive gas discharge. Phys. Lett. A; 2007, 361, 167–172.

2010 V.P. Torchigin V.P., A.V. Torchigin On phenomenon of light radiation from miniature balls immersed in water, Physics Letters A 374 (2010) 588-591

2010 V.P. Torchigin, A.V. Torchigin Ball Lightning as an Optical Incoherent Space Spherical Soliton. In Handbook of Solitons: Research, Technology and Applications. Editors S.P. Lang and Salim H. Bedore. Novapublishers (2010) 3-54

2011 V.P. Torchigin, A.V. Torchigin Chapter 6 Ball Lightning as an Optical Incoherent Space Spherical Soliton. In book Lightning: Properties, Formation and Types Editor Matthew D. Wood Novapublishers (2011) 133-184.

2012 Torchigin V.P., Torchigin A.V. Comparison of various approaches to the calculation of optically induced forces, Annals of Physics,Volume 327, Issue 9, September 2012, Pages 2288–2300 2012

2012 Torchigin V.P., Torchigin A.V. Interrelation between striction forces in dielectrics and optically induced forces in transparent media Physica Scripta Volume 86 Number 2 2012 86 025402

2013 Torchigin V.P., Torchigin A.V. Comment on ``Transverse radiation force in a tailored optical fiber" Physical Review A 2013 Vol. 88 p. 027801 013Torchigin V.P., Torchigin A.V. Compensation of the optically induced Lorentz force in a homogeneous optical medium Optik2013 Vol.124, p.5492-5495

2013 Torchigin V.P., Torchigin A.V. Interrelation between Ball Lightning and optically induced forces. PhysicaScripta013 Vol.88 number 3, p. 035402

2014 Torchigin V.P., Torchigin A.V. Optically induced force in a curve lightguide. EPJ AP European physical journal Applied Physics 2013, vol. 63, p. 10501

2014 Torchigin V.P., Torchigin A.V. Comment on "Theoretical analysis of the force on the end face of a nanofilament exerted by an outgoing light pulse" Physical Review A 2014, vol. 89, page 057801

2014 Torchigin V.P., Torchigin A.V. Magnitude of the photon momentum in matter. American Journal of Science and Technology 2014 Vol.4 Nom. 4 page 151-156

2014 Torchigin V.P., Torchigin A.V. Pressure Exerted on a Semi-Infinite Lossles Dispersionless Dielectric by a Plane Electromagnetic Wave OPEN JOURNAL OF MODERN PHYSICS 2014 Vol. nom. 3 1 page 1-7.

2014 Torchigin V.P., Torchigin A.V. Propagation of a light pulse inside matter in a context of the Abraham–Minkowski dilemma Optik 2014 vol. 125, issue 11, pp. 2687-2691.

2014 Torchigin V.P., Torchigin A.V. Resolution of the Age-Old Dilemma about a Magnitude of the Momentum of Light in Matter Physics Research International 2014, Vol. 2014, Pages 126436.

2014 Torchigin V.P., Torchigin A.V. The momentum of an electromagnetic wave inside a dielectric derived from the Snell refractive law Annals of Physics 2014, vol. 351, pages 444-446

Bychkov V. L. Bychkov A. V., Timofeev I. B J. Tech Fiz 2004, 74, issue 1, 128–133.

Dmitriev M. T. Priroda 1967, 6, 98.

Klimov, A. I.; Mishin, G. I. Letters in J. Tech. Fiz. 1993. 18 (13), 19.

Klimov, A., I.; Malchenko, D. M.; Sukovatkin, N.,N. In Ball lightning in laboratory; Avramenko R. F.; Ed.; Himiya: Moscow, 1994.

Sagan P Ball Lightning: Paradox of physics 2004 Lincoln, NJ.

Singer, S. The Nature of Ball Lightning; Plenum Press: NY, 1971.

Stakhanov I. P. The physical nature of Ball Lightning (Atomizdat, Moscow 1979 CEGB trans CE 8244)

Stenhoff M. Ball Lightning – An Unsolved problem in Atmospheric Physics, Plenum PNY, 1999.

TORCHIGIN V. AND TORCHIGIN A.